Pilot's
Cross-Country Guide to

NATIONAL PARKS AND HISTORICAL MONUMENTS

Vici and Warren DeHaan

TAB BOOKS Inc.
Blue Ridge Summit, PA

FIRST EDITION
FIRST PRINTING

Copyright © 1988 by TAB BOOKS Inc.
Printed in the United States of America

Library of Congress Cataloging in Publication Data

DeHaan, Vici.
Pilot's cross-country guide to national parks and historical
monuments / by Vici and Warren DeHaan.
p. cm.
Includes index.
ISBN 0-8306-2413-9 (pbk.)
1. National parks and reserves—United States—Guide-books.
2. United States—Description and travel—1981—Guide-books.
3. Air pilots—Travel—United States—Guide-books. 4. National
monuments—United States—Guide-books. I. DeHaan, Warren
V. (Warren Verne), 1940- . II. Title.
E160.D45 1988
917.3′04927—dc 19   88-11794
                                                              CIP

TAB BOOKS Inc. offers software for sale. For information and a catalog, please contact TAB
Software Department, Blue Ridge Summit, PA 17294-0850.

Questions regarding the content of this book
should be addressed to:

    Reader Inquiry Branch
    TAB BOOKS Inc.
    Blue Ridge Summit, PA 17294-0214

Contents

Introduction

"He who knows only his own generation remains always a child." This inscription over the entrance to CU's library in Boulder, Colorado, has always intrigued us. That's why taking a step back into the past while researching this book has produced an even greater awareness and understanding of just who we are as Americans and how we got to where we are today.

As we visited the historical sites scattered throughout the United States, we began to more fully appreciate the turmoil our country has gone through, as well as the divisiveness created by the Civil War. It's one thing to read about the various battles in the history books, but it's quite another to visit personally where the bitter fighting occurred.

Then, listening to naturalists tell about the lives of the early presidents and other historic people, such as Thomas Edison, was also fascinating. We were particularly enthralled by the naturalist at the Adams House National Historic Site. She had spent many hours reading about the Adams family, and for three spellbinding hours we felt totally removed from the Twentieth Century.

As you do your own explorations into the past, you might do it as we did—in a totally random fashion. We would select a direction of flight depending largely upon where we hadn't been before, and then find out what there was to see. However, it might be more fun to fly with a theme in mind.

Our country owes a great deal to its early leaders, and many historic sites have been set aside so the visitor can walk where the great once walked. Even though it's a reconstruction, we came away with a much better feel for Theodore Roosevelt, the man and the president, after visiting his boyhood home in New York City. We never realized that an unsuccessful assassination attempt had been made on his life, but his shirt, complete with bullet hole, proved it.

Other famous Americans include Thomas Jefferson, George Washington, and Abraham Lincoln, whose memorials are in Washington, D.C. Lincoln is also honored with three other historic sites: Lincoln Home National Historic Site in Illinois, Lincoln Boyhood National Monument in Indiana, and the Abraham Lincoln Birthplace National Historic Site in Kentucky.

You can also tour the Herbert Hoover National Historic Site in Iowa and the birthplaces of John Adams and John Quincy Adams, plus the JFK National Historic Site, in Massachussets. Clara Barton National Historic Site is in Maryland, and Saint-Gaudens National Historic Site is in New Hampshire.

In New York, you can tour the Roosevelt-Vanderbilt National Historical Site. The LBJ National Historic Park is in Texas; Eisenhower's National Historic Site is in Pennsylvania; Andrew Jackson's is in Tennessee; and George Washington's birthplace is in Virginia.

Other famous early Americans include Thomas Edison, whose National Historic Site is in New Jersey. Carl Sandburg's home is in North Carolina, and the Will Rogers Memorial is in Oklahoma. Booker T. Washington's National Monument is in Virginia; one for Benjamin Franklin is in Pennsylvania; and Roger Williams National Monument is in Rhode Island.

For pilots, an absolute must is the Wright Brothers National Monument in North Carolina. Most of us know about their early flights, but we found the magnitude of ideas they generated to be mind-boggling.

If you want to see some early settlements, visit Bent's Old Fort in Colorado, Homestead National Monument of America in Nebraska, San Antonio Missions National Historic Park in Texas, and the Historic Triangle of Jamestown, Yorktown, and Williamsburg in Virginia.

Memorials to early explorers can be found in California, where Cabrillo National Monument is located. The De Soto National Monument is in Florida, and Father Marquette's is in Michigan.

If you're a Civil War buff, you could begin your tour at Ft. Sumter National Monument in South Carolina, then fly a loop, stopping at the various battlefields: Antietam National Battlefield in Maryland; Vicksburg National Military Park in Mississippi; Gettysburg National Monument in Pennsylvania; Chickamauga and Chattanooga National Military Park, and Kennesaw Mountain National Battlefield Park in Georgia; Pea Ridge National Park in Arkansas; Harpers Ferry National Historic Park in West Virginia; Shiloh National Military Park in Tennessee; and Fredericksburg and Spotsylvania National Military Park, Manassas National Battlefield Park, and Petersburg National Battlefield in Virginia. You could end your tour at the Appomattox Court House National Historic Park in Virginia, where the hostilities finally ended.

Perhaps tracing the American Revolution sounds interesting to you. If you want to start at this war's beginning, go to the Minute Man National Historical Park in Massachussets, where colonists fired "the shot heard 'round the world." Be sure to visit Independence Hall in Pennsylvania, where the First Continental Congress met and where

Patrick Henry declared, "I know not what course others will take, but as for me, give me liberty, or give me death!"

Visit Saratoga in New York, where the British strategy of dividing their forces led to their defeat and where Burgoyne surrendered in 1777. Stop by Valley Forge National Historical Park in Pennsylvania, where Washington's army spent an incredible winter. Be sure to tour Yorktown Battlefield in Virginia, where Cornwallis' forces surrendered in 1781. Morristown National Historical Park in New Jersey is the site of the Continental Army's winter quarters for two years.

If the gold rush sounds like fun, visit Klondike Gold Rush National Historical Park in Alaska and the other one in Washington. You can also visit Death Valley National Monument in California, or Virginia City, Nevada.

If Indian history fascinates you, you can keep yourself occupied for days touring the various sites in the southwest. In Arizona, you can see Canyon de Chelly National Monument, Montezuma Castle National Monument, Sunset Crater National Monument, Wupatki National Monument, or Walnut Canyon National Monument. Visiting Colorado's Mesa Verde is also a must.

Other historic Indian ruins and historic sites include Ocmulgee National Monument, Georgia; Nez Perce National Historical Park, Idaho; Effigy Mounds National Monument, Iowa; Pipestone National Monument, Minnesota; Natchez Trace Parkway, Mississippi and Tennessee; Big Hole Battlefield National Monument and Custer Battlefield National Monument in Montana; Aztec Ruins National Monument, Bandelier and Chaco Culture National Historic Parks in New Mexico; Mound City Group National Monument in Ohio, and Blue Mounds State Park in Wisconsin.

The sites mentioned in this book were not meant to be all-inclusive, but were intended to be representative of what is available to the traveler. If we've left out one of your favorites you would like to see included, please let us know through the publisher. This is a large country to cover, and time simply doesn't permit us to do it all.

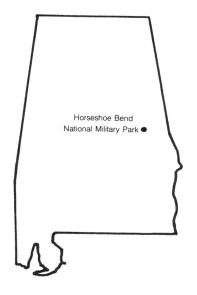

Horseshoe Bend
National Military Park ●

Alabama

HORSESHOE BEND NATIONAL MILITARY PARK

The park is 12 miles north of Dadeville and 18 miles northeast of Alexander City.

Airport

Alexander City, Atlanta Sectional
Latitude: 32–55
Longitude: 85–58
FSS: 1-800-392-5677
Car rentals:
    Avis: 205-234-2183

Accommodations

    Horseshoe Bend Motel: 205-234-6311
    Bob White Motel: 205-234-4215

In Dadeville:
    Still Waters Resort on Lake Martin, restaurant:
      205-825-7867

    Camping: Wind Creek State Park near Lake Martin, 6 miles south of Alexander City.

Features

    On the park site on March 27, 1814, Andrew Jackson's troops defeated approximately 1,000 Creek Indians led by Chief Menawa. As a result of the battle, the Creek Indian's power was broken over the southeastern United States. Land formerly occupied by these Indians included three-fifths of Alabama and one-fifth of Georgia.

    Jackson's victory helped build his national reputation. Nine months later he defeated the British in the Battle of New Orleans, ending the War of 1812. By 1829, he was elected president.

Activities

    A three-mile road loops through the battlefield, with six stops explaining the encounter. Thirteen miles of hiking trails lace the park, including a 2.8-mile nature trail through the battlefield.

    Watch Flintlock rifle demonstrations by a ranger in Tennessee Militia costume.

    Go boating or fishing in Lake Martin.

Information

Superintendent
Horseshoe Bend National Military Park
Rt. 1, P.O. Box 103
Daviston, AL 36256
205-234-7111

ALASKA

ADMIRALTY ISLAND NATIONAL MONUMENT

The monument is part of the Tongass National Forest. It is accessible by floatplane from either Juneau or Sitka, or through the Alaska Marine Highway System ferry.

Airports

Juneau International, Juneau Sectional
Latitude: 58–21
Longitude: 134–35
FSS: 907-789-7821
Car rentals

Sitka, Juneau Sectional
Latitude: 57–03
Longitude: 135–22
FSS: 907-966-2960
Car rentals: 907-966-2552

Accommodations

In Juneau:
 Tides Motel: 907-586-2452
 Baranof Hotel: 907-586-2660

 Breakwater Inn: 907-586-6303
 Sheffield Cape Fox: 907-586-6900

In Sitka:
 Sheffield Sitka: 907-747-6616
 Shee Atika Lodge: 907-747-6241

You can also stay in the rustic Forest Service cabins.

Features

The monument is a barrier island hosting the resident brown bears and nesting eagles. It features coastal rain forests of Sitka spruce, western hemlock, and thickets of wild currant and berries. The higher elevations have alpine meadows, lakes, and streams.

The Tlingit Indians and their ancestors have resided there for over a thousand years. They referred to the area as the *Xootsnoown*, or "Fortress of the Bears." Even today the park's population of brown bear outnumbers man. The Indians today live in the village of Angoon on the west coast.

Activities

Visitors can see the weathered remnants of whaling structures, canneries and old cabins.

You can traverse the island via an inland water trail from Seymour Canal to Mitchell Bay, or take a four-day canoe trip around the island.

Information

Admiralty Island National Monument
U.S.D.A. Forest Service
P.O. Box 2097
Juneau, AK 99803

BARROW

Although not a national park or monument, many pilots and visitors to Alaska want to visit Barrow, known as the "Top of the World."

Airport

Wiley Post-Will Rogers Memorial Airport, Barrow Sectional
Latitude: 71–17
Longitude: 156–45
FSS: 907-852-2511
Taxi

Accommodations

Brower's Hotel: 907-852-6231
Top of the World Hotel, restaurant:
  907-852-3900

Features

Barrow is the whaling capital of the Arctic. The sun doesn't set for 82 days during the summer: from May 10 to August 2. Then it doesn't rise for 67 days during the winter.

Barrow has the largest Eskimo village in North America. The Eskimos there still maintain a subsistence way of life with hunting, fishing, and whaling. They use ice cellars dug out of the permafrost to store their whale meat, fish, caribou, seal, and walrus. The Eskimos still use the walrus skin boat— but now it's powered with an outboard motor.

Activities

You can see the Eskimo Blanket Toss and other Eskimo ceremonial dances if your timing is right, or get some good pictures of the Arctic ice pack.

The Nalukatak Whaling Festival is celebrated at the end of the whaling season in June.

Visit the Post-Rogers Memorial found at the airport across the street from the Wien terminal. The memorial commemorates the deaths of Will Rogers and his pilot, Wiley Post, killed in 1935 in a plane crash 12 miles from there.

CAPE KRUSENSTERN NATIONAL MONUMENT

The monument is in northwest Alaska. It borders the Chukchi Sea and Kotzebue Sound. It is north of the Arctic Circle, and 450 miles northwest of Fairbanks. Its closest point is 10 miles northwest of Kotzebue.

Airport

Kotzebue-Ralph Wien Memorial, Nome Sectional
Latitude: 66–53
Longitude: 162–36
FSS: 907-442-3310

Access from Kotzebue is by chartered aircraft or boat. Wheeled planes land on primitive airstrips within the monument or along the beaches. Float-equipped planes land on the lagoons. Weather can make flying chancy.

Climate

The monument has long, cold winters and short, cool summers. The temperatures in June through August range from 40 to 65° F. June and July are the clearest months, but you'll find dense fog along the coast.

Accommodations

Closest accommodations are in Kotzebue's hotel: Nul-Luk-Vik, 442-3331. Otherwise, you can camp in the monument.

Features

The monument has 114 successive gravel layers rising from the sea that contain artifacts from every known Eskimo occupation of North America. These marine beach ridges are along the coast of the Chukchi Sea. They are the result of the beach-building process over 5,000 years.

The area is still inhabited by Eskimos, who continue to carry on their subsistence hunting, fishing, and gathering as they have for thousands of years.

The grizzly bear is common in the monument. It's legal to carry firearms for protection.

Activities

There are no ranger stations or visitor centers in the monument. Park rangers do patrol the area, however.

Visitors come primarily to backpack and camp. The best areas are on the coast on the west side or in the hills running north and south. You should check with the park service authorities prior to coming to the monument.

Mosquitoes appear in late June and are worst in July. They disappear in August. They are most dense in the interior lowlands. Be sure to carry repellent and possibly a head net for protection.

Information

Superintendent
National Park Service
Northwest Alaska Areas
P.O. Box 287
Kotzebue, AK 99752
907-442-3890

JUNEAU

Juneau lies along the Gastineau Channel. It is nestled at the foot of Mt. Robert and Mt. Juneau.

Airport

Juneau International, Juneau Sectional
Latitude: 58–21
Longitude: 134–35
FSS: 907-789-7821
Car rentals

Season

Visit Juneau between May and September. July is the warmest month; October is the wettest. Average daytime temperatures are mild. Expect rain, but do as the Alaskans do: Ignore it.

Accommodations

Tides Motel: 907-586-2452
Baranof Hotel: 907-586-2660
Breakwater Inn: 907-586-6303
Sheffield Cape Fox: 907-586-6900

Camping: Campgrounds in the area vary from commercial to "do-what-you-please." Cabins on the Chilkoot are for drying out only.

Features

The Mendenhall Glacier was left from the Little Ice Age that began 3,000 years ago. The glacier was formed from snow that falls on the 1,500-square-mile Juneau Icefield. The ice flows down the valley for 12 miles, almost reaching the visitor center.

Activities

Juneau has one of the most extensive hiking trail networks in Alaska. You can take an easy 1-hour hike up Basin Road to the AJ mine ruins, or climb to the top of Mt. Juneau.

Hitchhiking is legal. Many of the trailheads are within walking distance of the ferry landings.

You can rent a bike and cycle out to the Mendenhall, 8 miles out of town. There you can hike beside the glacier, following marked hiking trails, which go down both sides. You can also hike south out of town to see the huge crushing and recovery mill, which is the terminus for 300 miles of tunnels through which $80 million in gold was extracted.

Take a walking tour of the city. A good guide to purchase is Mike Miller's *So This Is Juneau*.

Charter a floatplane from Glacier Bay Airways or Southeast Skyways to fly over the 1,500-square-mile Juneau Icefield and the Taku Glacier.

Attend the brown-bag luncheon concert performed on a 548-pipe organ on Friday afternoons on the eighth floor of the State Office Building, often referred to as the SOB.

Tour the House of Wickersham or visit the Alaska State Museum to see Indian and Eskimo artifacts.

KOBUK VALLEY NATIONAL PARK

The park is 40 miles north of the Arctic Circle, 350 miles northwest of Fairbanks, and 75 miles east of Kotzebue. It's ringed on the north by the Baird Mountains and to the south by the Waring Mountains. Prior to visiting this park, you're advised to visit with the National Park Service in Kotzebue.

Airports

Kotzebue-Ralph Wien Memorial, Nome Sectional
Latitude: 66–53
Longitude: 162–36
FSS: 907-442-3310

From this airport you can take a charter flight into the park. You also can get charters from Am-bler and Kiana, but you'll need to make prior arrangements. Aircraft fly into primitive airstrips within the park or land on sandbars.

Ambler Airport, Fairbanks Sectional
Latitude: 67–06
Longitude: 157–51
FSS: 907-442-3147

Climate

This area's climate is generally dry and cold. Summer temperatures in the dunes area can exceed 100° F. The weather is clearest during June and July. The rain increases in August and September.

Mosquitoes are out in late June, and are at their worst in July but gone by August. They are most dense in the wet lowlands and less thick in the drier highlands.

Accommodations

In Kotzbue:
  Nul-Luk-Vik Hotel, restaurant, 907-442-3331

There are some accommodations in Kiana, but none in Ambler. Both towns have some small stores, so you're advised to do your major purchasing in either Fairbanks (Fig. 1) or Anchorage. Camping is in primitive sites.

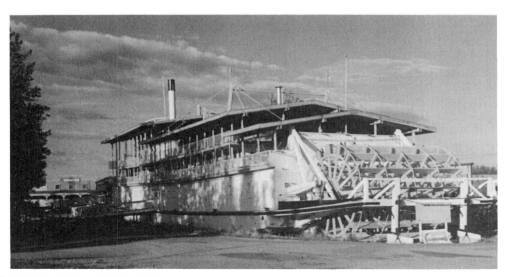

Fig. 1. Paddlewheeler on display at Fairbanks.

Features

Great herds of caribou cross the Kobuk River at Onion Portage. These same herds once fed the Woodland Eskimo people living there in 1250 A.D. Human occupation of the portage has been dated back to 12,500 years ago.

The area also features 25 square miles of sand dunes, the Great Kobuk Sand Dunes, located south of the Kobuk River. These dunes rise as high as 100 feet. The dunes are the largest active dune fields in the Arctic latitudes. They were formed from sand blown in from the mountains to the north. They date back to 33,000 years ago.

Activities

It's a great place for canoeing and kayaking. Follow the Kobuk River, which flows for 300 miles, starting from the south flank of the Brooks Range and ending up in Kotzebue Sound and the Chukchi Sea.

You can visit several Eskimo villages located along the Kobuk, take float trips along the Kobuk River or Salmon River, fish, or walk on the dunes, which are reached by an easy hike from the river. Backpackers can hike into the park from either Ambler or Kiana.

Information

Superintendent
National Park Service
Northwest Alaska Areas
P.O. Box 287
Kotzbue, AK 99752
907-442-3890

MISTY FJORDS NATIONAL MONUMENT

Misty Fjords is located east of Ketchikan.

Airport

Ketchikan, Ketchikan Sectional
Latitude: 55–21
Longitude: 131–43

FSS: 907-225-9481
Car rentals: 907-225-5123

Accommodations

Marine View, restaurant: 907-225-6601
Hilltop Motel: 907-225-5166
Super 8: 907-225-9088
Ingersoll Hotel: 907-225-2124

The U.S. Forest Service also maintains 15 wilderness cabins.

Climate

The area is generally overcast and rainy. Ketchikan receives 160 inches of annual rainfall.

Features

The monument has over 100 lakes, many teeming with trout. All five species of Pacific salmon spawn in the streams within the monument. Rudyard Bay has very steep shoreline walls, which rise 3,000 feet.

Ketchikan is a fishing, lumbering village almost 4 miles long and in places is one street deep. The houses and shops are built on stilts along the water side of the street because of the shortage of flat land. Ketchikan has the largest collection of totem poles in the world.

Activities

You can cruise out of Ketchikan through the fjords to see the New Eddystone Rock, a 237-foot island formation visited by Captain George Vancouver in 1793. It was named for its resemblance to the lighthouse off Plymouth.

Ride aboard Misty Fjord's 50 footer, which carries passengers within the monument daily except Sundays. Cruise into Rudyard Bay with its vertical rock walls and be treated to a great view of its many waterfalls.

Take a flight via floatplane from Ketchikan to the luxury fishing resort at Waterfall. From here, 21-foot cabin cruisers take you fishing for king salmon which can weigh up to 60 pounds, or for 15 pound silver salmon.

On July 4, the Logging Carnival takes place, with local loggers testing their skills. In August, the area holds a Blueberry Festival.

NOATAK NATIONAL PRESERVE

The preserve is located 70 miles from Kotzebue with the Gates of the Arctic located on its eastern boundary.

Airport

Kotzebue-Ralph Wien Memorial, Nome Sectional
Latitude: 66–53
Longitude: 162–36
FSS: 907-442-3310

From there, get a charter flight or arrange for a chartered boat ride into the preserve.

Climate

The area experiences long, cold winters and short, mild summers. Mid-summer temperatures average in the 60s and 70s, but it can dip below freezing on summer nights. June is the clearest. July and August have increasing cloudiness. Summer fog is generally found along the coast and in Kotzebue.

Season

The river is open by June 1. It's highest then and there are no biting insects. The midnight sun provides long hours of light. July offers many wildflowers—and, unfortunately, many mosquitoes. The river levels rise and fall depending upon the rainfall.

August is a good month to visit for good berry picking and not as many biting insects.

All river floaters should plan to be off the river by September 20 to avoid the river's freeze-up.

Accommodations

No accommodations are available in the preserve. You'll need to stay in Kotzebue:
Nul-Luk-Vik: 442-3331

Features

Glacier-fed headwaters of the river are located in Gates of the Arctic. You'll see the fastest and most hazardous water there. The middle section of the river averages 5 to 8 mph. The lower part below Kelly River is slow and braided.

The area also contains some 200 archeological sites, with some dating back 5,000 years.

Activities

Two ranger stations are located in the area. One is on the Upper Noatak River, approximately 10 miles west of Douglas Creek. The other is on Noatak River, 1½ miles upriver from the Kelly River.

Floaters usually average 20 to 25 miles per day. The preserve has approximately 250 miles of rivers to float. Be prepared for fog and wind, as well as below-freezing temperatures.

Be sure to bring along sufficient food to cope with delayed flights because of the weather.

Information

Noatak National Preserve
National Park Service
Kotzebue, AK 99752
907-442-3890

SITKA NATIONAL MONUMENT

Sitka is in Alaska's southeastern panhandle.

Airport

Sitka, Juneau Sectional
Latitude: 57–03
Longitude: 135–22
FSS: 907-966-2221
Car rentals: 907-966-2552

Climate

Expect frequent rain in the summer, with temperatures ranging in the 50s and 60s. Annual precipitation averages 95 inches.

Accommodations

Shee Atika Lodge, 907-747-6241
Sheffield House, 907-747-6616 or 800-544-0970
Sitka Hotel, 907-747-3285

In Glennallen:
Ahtna Lodge, 907-822-3288

In Tok:
Tundra Lodge, 907-262-9169

Additional accommodations are available along the Glenn and Richardson Highways, and along the road to Tok.

Camping: 20 campgrounds are located on Baranof Chicagof and Kruzof Islands. Access is by boat or floatplane. Contact the U.S. Forest Service, Sitka District Ranger, P.O. Box 504, ATD, Sitka, AK 99835, 747-6671.

Note: Bears and bugs are quite abundant in the area. Be prepared with plenty of insect repellent. Some visitors also carry a .30-06 caliber rifle for protection.

The major fishing camps are: Tanada, Copper Lakes, Ptarmigan Lake, Rock Lake, Tebaz, and Hanagitoc Lake. There are rustic accommodations at McCarthy, Kennicott, and at Ptarmigan Lake Lodge.

Features

The early Tlingit Indians followed the salmon to Sitka to settle at *Shee Atika*. However, their settlement was visited in 1804 by Alexander Baranov, head of the Russian-American Company. This Russian colonial outpost's foundries cast some of the bells now found in Padre Serra's California missions.

A battle ensued and the Tlingit were defeated when they ran out of ammunition and withdrew. Baranov then burned their fort and rebuilt a new town, which he called New Archangel. This battle marked the northwest coast natives' last major resistance to the coming of the white man.

St. Michael's Cathedral, a Russian orthodox church built in the 1840s, was destroyed by fire in 1966. Fortunately, many of the icons and artifacts were saved and can still be seen.

The totem pole seen in the park was carved by the Haida Indians, who lived further south.

Mt. Edgecombe, 3,271 feet, is an extinct volcano that closely resembles Mt. Fujiyama.

Activities

Take an evening or Sunday afternoon cruise with Foolish Pleasure Cruises, 747-8740.

Visit Castle Hill, site of the first raising of the Stars and Stripes when the United States purchased Russian America from czarist Russia in 1867. It's a national historic landmark and provides a great overlook of the surrounding area. There the first 49-star flag was raised when Alaska became a state in 1959.

Tour Totem Pole Park to see 14 totem poles, both replicas and originals. Also visit the site of the old Tlingit fort and location of the memorable battle of 1804 between the Indians and Alexander Baranov's men.

Take a stroll along two miles of walkways that pass through the spruce-hemlock forest. The path is lined with tall trees and totem poles and has several picnicking facilities.

The Sitka area has 40 established trails in the vicinity. Rubber boots are a necessity for a more enjoyable hike.

You can go fishing in five lakes: Beaver, Salmon, Gut Bay Lake, Dedrickson, and Lower Goulding Lake. The first two are too small to be reached by floatplane, but are accessible on foot by trail or by skiff. The others are accessible by plane.

See the New Archangel Folk Dancers. This troupe presents Russian folk dances from various regions of Russia. Their performances are timed to coincide with the docking of cruise ships or by special arrangement. For information, write: P.O. Box 1687, ATD, Sitka, AK 99835.

The SARAC Folkdance/Folklore Festival features a week-long adult camp in June where you can participate in dances and cultures from all over the world. Contact the SARAC Folk Dance Festival at 907-747-8177.

The Sitka Summer Music Festival is held the first three weeks in June. It features musicians from the U.S. and Europe, who present seven classical concerts. Contact the Chairman, Sitka Summer Music Festival, P.O. Box 907-ATD, Sitka, or call 907-747-6774.

The All-Alaska Logging Championships are held in late June and feature the World Championship Hooktenders Race.

Flying Service for hunting and fishing is available from Bellair, P.O. Box 371, 475 Katlian, Sitka, 99835, 907-747-8636.

Information

Chamber of Commerce
P.O. Box 638
Sitka, AK 99835
907-747-8604

''Cabins and Trails'' information
Forest Service
Sitka, AK 99835

KLONDIKE GOLD RUSH NATIONAL HISTORICAL PARK

The park is in Skagway, located on the northernmost section of the Inside Passage.

Airport

Skagway Airport, Juneau Sectional
Latitude: 59–27
Longitude: 135–19
907-983-2323

Car rentals:
    Avis, Klondike Hotel: 907-983-2347
    National Car Rental: 907-983-2451 or
        907-983-2294
    Taxi: Goldies: 907-983-2321
    Golden North: 907-983-2451
    Koster's Cab: 907-983-2636

Climate

The area is generally mild and fairly dry. Annual precipitation is less than 29 inches. It receives more sunshine than any other southeastern Alaskan town.

Accommodations

5th Avenue Bunkhouse: 907-983-2370
Gold Rush Motel: 907-983-2631
Golden North Motel: 907-983-2451
Skagway Inn: 907-983-2289

Camping: Hanousek Park, Lionsville State Campground, and Dyea Campground.

Features

The city of Skagway was named after the Tlingit word *Skagun*, meaning windy place. During the gold rush of 1898, it grew into the largest town in Alaska, with a population of about 10,000.

Activities

The Klondike Gold Rush National Historical Park also includes Skagway Historical District's seven-block stretch of historical buildings. The visitors center has naturalists who are available to accompany you on short walking tours.

Walk through town to see its many reminders of the gold rush days. The town has many of the original falsefront buildings and wooden boardwalks. Stop by the Gold Rush Cemetery to see the graves of Soapy Smith and Frank Reid, who dueled with Smith.

You can also hike several trails: Dewey Lakes Trail system, Skyline Trail to A.B. Mountain, and the most famous trail: Chilkoot Trail, 33 miles long, following the trek of the gold seekers from Dyea to Lake Bennett. Hikers should be prepared for a wide range of temperatures and weather, including snow, rain, fog, wind, snowfields, and swamps.

It's recommended that you hike north from the ghost town of Dyea to get the feel of the route of the early miners. The opposite direction isn't recommended because of the very steep scree slope near the summit, "The Golden Stairs." If you watch the movies at the visitors center, you'll get a better understanding of this advice. The hike requires 3 to 5 days.

You can also drive over White Pass via the Klondike Highway, or go by bus twice daily up the South Klondike Highway to Whitehorse.

Skagway Charters offers flightseeing trips to Glacier Bay and the Gold Rush Trail of '98. Contact them at P.O. Box 307, Skagway, AK 99840.

A cruise down the Inside Passage from Skagway brings you into Glacier Bay with its 16 large glaciers.

Information

Superintendent
Klondike Rush National Historical Park
P.O. Box 517
Skagway, AK 99840
907-983-2400
or
Seattle, WA 98104
206-442-7220

WRANGELL-ST. ELIAS NATIONAL PARK AND PRESERVE

The park is located in the Yukon Territory adjacent to Canada's Kluane National Park, where the Wrangell St. Elias and Chugach mountain ranges converge. It includes ten of the highest peaks on the continent.

Airports

Wrangell, Juneau Sectional
Latitude: 56–29
Longitude: 132–22
FSS: 907-966-2221
Car rentals: 907-874-3322

Yakutat, Juneau Sectional
Latitude: 59–30
Longitude: 139–40
FSS: 907-784-3314

Gulkana, Anchorage Sectional
Latitude: 62–09
Longitude: 145–27
FSS: 907-822-3236
Car rentals

You can get chartered flights from Anchorage, Fairbanks, Northway, Glennallen, Cordova, Valdez, or Yakutat. Air access into the park from Gulkana Airport is provided by Ellis Air Taxi or Sportsman's Flying Service.

Access

Two bus lines provide access to Glennallen near the park. The Anchorage-Valdez Bus Line leaves the Captain Cook Hotel daily except Monday at 8:00 A.M.

Alaska-Yukon Motorcoaches leave the Sheffield House at 9:00 A.M. on Sunday, Tuesday, Thursday, and Saturday.

From Glennallen, roads into the park are either the Chitina-McCarthy Road or the Nabesna Road from Slana to Nabesna. The McCarthy Road goes 65 miles up the Chitina River Valley from Chitina to the Kennicott River. It's generally passable during the summer, but the road isn't regularly maintained, so be sure to get current road conditions prior to leaving.

Accommodations

Roadhouse Lodge: 907-874-2335
Car rentals
Stikine Inn: 907-874-3388 or 89
Ahtna Lodge: 907-822-3289
Yakutat Airport Lodge: 907-784-3232
Glacier Bear Lodge: 907-784-3202

You can also stay in Forest Service cabins accessible by floatplane. Contact Forest Service Wrangell District Ranger, P.O. Box 51, ATD, Wrangell, AK 99929, 907-874-2323.

Camping: Liberty Creek near Chiltna and Sourdough north of Gulkana. Campgrounds are also located along the Richardson Highway, Tok Cutoff, and Edgerton Highway. Purchase your supplies in Glenallen. A limited amount is available at McCarthy.

Climate

The summers are cool, cloudy, and rainy, which can interfere with scheduled pickups by chartered planes. You'll experience some hot, clear days in July, when the weather is best. August is cool and wet, but has fewer mosquitoes. Winters are cold and dark, with temperatures dropping to $-50°$ F.

Features

Wrangell is surrounded by fjords, dense forests, and rugged streams. Visit the beach at low tide so you can see *petroglyphs*, ancient rock carvings. They are estimated to be 8,000 years old.

The park preserves the largest number of glaciers and greatest number of peaks over 16,000 feet. One glacier, the Malaspina, is larger than the state of Rhode Island. Mount St. Elias is 18,008 feet, and is the second highest peak in the United States.

The Stikine River is the fastest navigable river in North America. It was the site of a small gold rush in 1861, when gold was found on the sandbars. This river has a 60-mile stretch that's called the "Grand Canyon on the Stikine."

Firearms are allowed in the park for defensive purposes. A healthy respect for the resident bears is essential.

Activities

Visit Bear Tribal House, a Tlingit tribal house of the Bear Clan on Chick Shakes Island. It features a good collection of totems, and is accessible from the mainland by a footbridge at the bottom of Front Street.

Visit two old mining towns: McCarthy and Kennicott.

Fish for king salmon, some weighing 50 pounds. Charter a floatplane for your fishing expedition. Then arrange to stay in the Forest Service cabins, also accessible by floatplane.

Wilderness backpacking, car camping, river running, and mountain climbing are available. However, the area's streams, rivers, and glaciers can present formidable barriers, and most of the trails depicted on the topographical maps are either unmaintained historic routes or suitable for winter travel only.

Information

Superintendent
Wrangell-St. Elias National Park and Preserve
P.O. Box 29
Glennallen, AK 99588
907-822-5234

Chamber of Commerce
P.O. Box 49
Wrangell, AK 99929
907-874-3068

Arizona

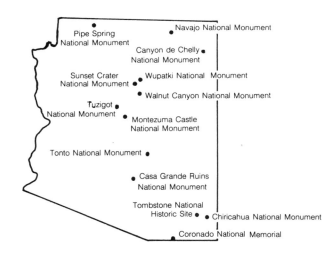

Pipe Spring National Monument

Navajo National Monument

Canyon de Chelly National Monument

Sunset Crater National Monument

Wupatki National Monument

Walnut Canyon National Monument

Tuzigot National Monument

Montezuma Castle National Monument

Tonto National Monument

Casa Grande Ruins National Monument

Tombstone National Historic Site

Chiricahua National Monument

Coronado National Memorial

CANYON DE CHELLY NATIONAL MONUMENT

To reach the monument from Gallup, go by way of Window Rock, Ganado and Chinle. A second route is from Holbrook or Kearns Canyon via Rt. 264 and Rt. 63 to Chinle. A third route goes from Kayenta via Mexico Water, Round Rock, and Many Farms to Chinle. The monument is 3 miles beyond Chinle.

Airports

Window Rock, Denver Sectional
Latitude: 35–39
Longitude: 109–04
FSS: 800-352-0512

Gallup Municipal, Albuquerque Sectional
Latitude: 35–30
Longitude: 108–47
FSS: 505-722-4308
Car rentals

Holbrook Municipal, Phoenix Sectional
Latitude: 34–56
Longitude: 110–08
Car rentals

Accommodations

Thunderbird Lodge in the monument. Reservations advisable: 602-638-2401
Canyon de Chelly Motel: 602-674-5288

In Gallup:
Best Western, The Inn, restaurant: 505-722-2221
El Capitan Motel, restaurant nearby: 505-863-6828
Gallup TraveLodge, restaurant nearby, open 24 hours: 505-863-9301
Holiday Inn, restaurant: 505-722-2201

In Kayenta:
Holiday Inn: 602-697-3221
Wetherill Inn Motel: 602-697-3231

In Window Rock:
Window Rock Motor Inn, next to the airport: 602-871-4108

Camping: No camping is allowed in the canyons, but you can camp year-round at Cottonwood Campground near Monument Headquarters. Campers are advised to bring their own fuel. Gas and food are available every day except Sunday at the nearby trading post.

Features

Canyon de Chelly contains five periods of Indian culture dating from 348 to 1300 A.D. The earliest were the Basketmakers, who constructed the sunken circular structures. The Anasazi, or Pueblo people, built the apartment-style homes in caves and rock shelters above the canyon floor. Most of the large cliff houses were constructed between 1100 and 1300 A.D.

The principal ruins are the White House, Antelope House, Standing Cave, and Mummy Cave. Mummy Cave has been tree-ring dated as far back as 348, and features a three-story tower house.

White House ruin was once believed to contain as many as 80 rooms. However, because of stream erosion, only 60 rooms and four kivas remain. White House was built between approximately 1040 and 1275 A.D., and was occupied by a maximum population of 50 to 60 people.

A prolonged drought in 1200 forced many of the people to abandon their homes. Currently, approximately 300 Navajos occupy summer homes in the canyon, utilizing the canyon floor for peach orchards, farming, and grazing. They live in hogans, and have become well-known for their hand-woven rugs and silver work.

Activities

As you drive to the canyon via the Window Rock route, be sure to watch for the natural rock formation for which the town of Window Rock was named. Also, if you're here early in September, attend their annual fair.

You'll pass Hubbell's Trading Post, designated as a National Historical Site. You can tour the Hubbell home to see a collection of Navajo rugs.

Visitors are only permitted to go into the canyons if accompanied by a park ranger or authorized guide because of the presence of quicksand, flash floods, and to protect the privacy of the Navajos who own the land. If you decide to photograph any

of them, it's customary to ask permission. A nominal fee is suggested.

The 24-mile paved road along the north rim of Canyon del Muerto offers four scenic overlooks. The 21-mile paved road along the south ruin has five overlooks and offers access to White House Trail.

One-mile-long White House Trail is one hike you can take without a guide. The trail head isn't marked, but is located approximately 150 yards from the parking lot and to the right of the overlook. As you descend, you pass rock formations of sand dunes, which once covered this area around 200 million years ago. Cross the river to reach the ruins. Be sure to carry drinking water. The water in the river is not drinkable.

The owners of the Thunderbird Lodge will arrange daily Jeep trips into the canyon from early April to October 31. You can take either a half or all-day trip. Reservations: 602-674-5443. If you decide to drive a four-wheel vehicle through the canyons, you must give a day's notice and arrange for a Navajo guide.

Information

Superintendent
Canyon de Chelly National Monument
P.O. Box 588
Chinle, AZ 86503
602-674-5436

CASA GRANDE RUINS NATIONAL MONUMENT

The ruins are located at the edge of the Pima Indian Reservation midway between Phoenix and Tucson, 1 mile north of Coolidge on Arizona 87.

Airports

Casa Grande Municipal, Phoenix Sectional
Latitude: 32–57
Longitude: 111–47
FSS: 505-723-3392
Car rentals

Casa Grande–Three Point, Phoenix Sectional
Latitude: 32–54
Longitude: 111–45
FSS: 505-889-9689
Ground transportation is available to Casa Grande from Three Point.

Tucson International, Phoenix Sectional
Latitude: 32–07
Longitude: 110–56
FSS: 602-889-9689
Car rentals:
    Hertz: 800-654-3131
    Avis: 800-331-2221

Season

Open year round with hours 7:00 A.M. to 6:00 P.M. daily. The best time to visit is from early October to early May. Summer temperatures can reach 120° F.

Accommodations

In Casa Grande:
    Francisco Grande Resort, restaurant: 602-836-8711
    Ramada Inn, restaurant: 505-836-5000
    Boots and Saddle Motel: 505-836-8249

In Florence:
    Blue Mist Motel: 505-683-2273

In Tucson:
    Best Western Ghost Ranch Lodge, restaurant: 602-751-7565
    Best Western Inn At the Airport, airport transportation: 602-746-0271
    Granada Royale Hometel, airport transportation, restaurant: 602-572-0700

Features

Casa Grande was probably built around 1350 A.D., and was occupied by the Gila Valley Pueblo people who built a solid mud four-story watchtower featuring some rather unusual building patterns.

First the occupants built 7-foot walls on which they constructed a three-story apartment. The upstairs apartments accommodated 11 families. The main building is surrounded by the remains of a walled village that once contained from 60 to 90 rooms.

Casa Grande contained a blend of two Indian cultures, the Hohokam and the Pueblo. The Hohokam Indians developed an extensive system of irrigation canals that made it possible for them to get water from the Gila River to farm the arid desert in which they lived.

Activities

Walk along the self-guided Casa Grande Trail, an easy walk of 400 yards.

The visitor center has interpretative exhibits. You can also attend ranger talks or picnic on the grounds.

Information

Superintendent
Casa Grande Ruins National Monument
P.O. Box 518
Coolidge, AZ 85228
602-723-3172

CHIRICAHUA NATIONAL MONUMENT

The monument is located in the southeast corner of Arizona, 36 miles from Willcox, and 70 miles northeast of Douglas. The county road is unpaved and can be rough in places. A mountainous route goes from Portal, but is difficult and not recommended for drivers not accustomed to mountain driving.

Airports

Bisbee Municipal, Phoenix Sectional
Latitude: 31–23
Longitude: 109–54
FSS: 800-352-0512
Car rentals

Willcox-Cochise County, Phoenix Sectional
Latitude: 32–16
Longitude: 109–54
FSS: 800-352-0512

Season

Temperatures are usually mild, but winter can be cold and unpredictable. Most precipitation is received in July and August. In July, the temperatures average 74° F; in January, 40° F.

Accommodations

There are no accommodations in the park.

In Bisbee:
Bisbee-Desert Inn: 602-364-8477
TraveLodge: 602-364-8434
San Jose Lodge, restaurant: 602-422-2226

In Willcox:
Siesta Motel: 602-384-3877
Imperial 400 Motel: 602-384-2237
TraveLodge: 602-384-2266

Camping in Willcox: KOA, Ft. Willcox and Sun Valley. National forest campgrounds near Willcox: Turkey Creek, Pinery Canyon and Rustler Peak.

There is a campground open year-round at 5,340 feet in Bonita Canyon near the headquarters.

Features

The monument was formed millions of years ago when nearby volcanoes erupted. The white-hot ash welded into rock and was later split by block faulting. Now you can see very slender, delicate needles of rhyolite stone. Seventeen miles of "mod" rock sculptures have been created from old lava flows that were piled up layer upon layer. This lava then shrank while cooling and vertical cracks were created. Later the earth was lifted, tilted, and eroded, undercutting the different rock layers.

Watch for the massive balanced rocks, such as Punch and Judy and the China Boys. Another formation, the Totem Pole, is 137 feet high and only measures 1 yard at its narrowest point. The Big Balanced Rock weighs 1,000 tons and is on a base that is only 4 feet thick.

The mountains were originally a fortress for the Chiricahua Apache. Their well-remembered leader, Cochise, helped make travel hazardous for passengers on the Butterfield Stage Line until a peace treaty was finally signed in 1886.

Along the skyline to the northeast you can see Cochise Head, an upturned profile of the famous chief. The formation is located in the 8,100-foot Chiricahua Mountains.

Activities

The Cochise Visitors Center is located 2 miles past the monument entrance. A special program is presented twice a week from early April through May, and from early June through mid-September.

Visit the Faraway Ranch to see how the early pioneers lived in the southwest.

You can drive 6½ miles on Massai Point Drive, a paved road that climbs up Bonita Canyon, passing through a bright red layer of ancient lake beds. Massai Point offers a good view of the monument. The Massai Point Trail is ½ mile long.

You can also visit an exhibit building to learn about the geology of the area. There is a ½-mile self-guided nature trail. You can also follow 17 miles of other trails in the monument including Heart of Rocks, 7 miles round-trip, which goes to Punch and Judy and the Big Balanced Rock.

Information

Park Superintendent
Chiricahua National Monument
Box 6500
Dos Cabezas Star Route
Willcox, AZ 85643
602-824-3560

Nearby Attractions

Ft. Bowie National Historic Site. To reach it, you must hike in 1½ miles beginning on Apache Pass. In 1862, the fort was the center of the military operations against Geronimo and his Apaches.

CORONADO NATIONAL MEMORIAL
AND
TOMBSTONE NATIONAL HISTORIC SITE

Coronado National Memorial is located at the southeast tip of Huachuca Mountains along the Mexican border in southeast Arizona. The closest town is Bisbee. The Montezuma Canyon Road leading into the monument joins SR 92 20 miles west of Bisbee. Tombstone is northeast of Coronado.

Airports

Bisbee Municipal, Phoenix Sectional
Latitude: 31–23
Longitude: 109–54
FSS: 800-352-0512
Car rentals

Tombstone Municipal, Phoenix Sectional
Latitude: 31–40
Longitude: 110–01
FSS: 800-352-0512

When we landed at Tombstone, we were met by the sheriff, who drove out to pick us up and bring us into town. He informed us that the residents of the city listened for when private aircraft arrived and tried to meet them and provide them with transportation to town.

If you happen to have bicycles along in the plane, the 4-mile trip into Tombstone is a nice ride.

Accommodations

In Bisbee:
San Jose Lodge, restaurant: 602-422-2226

In Willcox:
Best Western Desert Inn of Willcox: 602-384-3577
Best Western Plaza Inn, restaurant open 24 hours: 602-384-3556
El Dorado: 602-287-4611

In Tombstone:
Best Western Lookout Lodge: 602-457-2223 or 800-528-1234

Camping: No overnight camping is permitted in the memorial. However, there is a campground in neighboring Coronado National Forest.

Climate

Tombstone has become a year-round health resort because of its cool summers and moderate winters.

Features

The Coronado memorial commemorates the first extensive European penetration into North America led by Francisco Vasquez de Coronado in 1540 A.D. His large group of Spaniards, priests, and Mexican-Indians were searching for the Seven Cities of Cibola. However, five months of hard travel brought them into these rock pueblos built by the Zuni Indians. Despite finding no riches, their expedition did give new knowledge of the southwest and led to further exploration and settlement.

Tombstone is known as the "Town that is Too Tough to Die." It is probably one of Arizona's most famous silver mining camps. It was named by an early prospector, Ed Schieffelin, who was told that the only thing he could expect to find was his own tombstone. In 1877, he staked his first claim and called it Tombstone. Soon rumors of rich strikes followed, and days of lawlessness and violence followed. It was so rough that one of the first jobs of the local storekeeper was to sweep all the bodies off the walk in front of his store.

The mines in the area produced millions of dollars in gold and silver before they were forced to close because of rising underground water. Citizens were offered two kinds of burial services: "Tourist" or "First Class Deluxe" in which they removed your boots.

At the height of the hostilities, the famous Earp-Clanton gunfight was fought at the OK Corral.

Activities

Drive from the headquarters up to the Montezuma Pass parking area. There's an excellent overlook 3 miles west of Montezuma Pass.

One hike begins from the visitors center and goes 3 miles to Montezuma Pass, or take the short, self-guided trail to Coronado Peak, 6,864 feet, offering you a good overlook of the San Pedro River Valley. This trail begins at the shelter for Coronado Peak and has exhibits along the way pointing out information about Coronado's expedition, along with markers with quotes from his journals.

Hike 3 miles along Joe's Canyon Trail back to headquarters via Smugglers Ridge to see views of the Sonora to the south and San Pedro Valley to the east. Guided nature walks are available upon request.

If you're in the area in April, attend a pageant commemorating the Coronado expedition.

Activities in Tombstone: Visit the Boothill graveyard to see the graves of various badmen, one lynched victim, and the bodies of the mass execution of a quintet from Bisbee.

Visit some of the historic buildings such as the Crystal Palace, considered to be one of the most luxurious saloons in the west, Bird Cage Theater, and the Tombstone Epitaph Building.

If you visit the OK Corral, you'll see the place where the Earp- Clanton gunfight occurred on October 16, 1881. To see a live enactment of the gunfight, be there on either the first or third Sunday of the month. The "Vigilantes" put on an exhibition there the second and fourth Saturdays of the month.

The first week in March features Centennial Days. Wyatt Earp Days are the last weekend in May. Wild West Days are the first week in September, and Hellodorado Days occurs the third weekend in October.

Information

Park Superintendent
RR 1, Box 126
Hereford, AZ 85615
602-366-5515

MONTEZUMA CASTLE NATIONAL MONUMENT

The Castle is located 60 miles south of Flagstaff. Follow 89A through Sedona, or take Black Canyon, I-17, Highway 79, south for 60 miles from Flagstaff. The well is 11 miles northeast of the castle.

Airport

Pulliam, Phoenix Sectional
Latitude: 35–08
Longitude: 111–40
FSS: 800-352-0512
Car rentals:
    Avis: 602-774-8421
    Budget: 602-779-0306

Accommodations

In Flagstaff:
    Best Western Pony Soldier Motel:
        602-526-2388
    Arizonan Motel: 602-774-7171
    Quality Inn: 602-774-8771

In Sedona:
    Best Western Arroyo Roble Hotel:
        602-282-4001
    Quality Inn-King's Ransom Motor Hotel,
        restaurant: 602-282-7191
    Village Inn Motel: 602-282-7187

Campgrounds are located in Oak Creek Canyon, Clear and Beaver Creeks.

Features

Montezuma's Castle is actually misnamed since it's not a castle at all, but a large apartment house. The castle is one of the best preserved prehistoric cliff dwellings in the southwest.

In 700 A.D., the Hohokam lived in small clusters of one-room huts along the streambeds. About 350 years later, dry farming Sinagua Indians built small pueblos of stone. Around 1250 A.D., they built larger structures on the hilltops and in the cliffs, including two five-story apartment houses. One was Montezuma Castle, which had 20 rooms, and a nearby castle that had 45 or more rooms.

The cliff homes were occupied for approximately two centuries. By 1450, the castle had been deserted.

Montezuma Well is a large limestone sink 470 feet in diameter, with water 55 feet deep. You can also see their ancient irrigation ditches, cliff and hilltop houses built around the well.

Activities

The area has a visitors center. From here, you follow self-guided Sycamore Trail to get a look at the castle's 20-room, five-story apartment. Visitors to Montezuma Castle are not permitted inside because of the unstable nature of the building. However, you are permitted to visit the excavated lower rooms of Castle A, which includes a natural cave room.

When you go to the well, you can take a self-guided tour to see the Indian pueblos and cave houses on the rim. A paved walk leads down to the well and irrigation ditches.

Information

Superintendent
Montezuma Castle National Monument
P.O. Box 219
Camp Verde, AZ 86322
602-567-3322

NAVAJO NATIONAL MONUMENT

The monument is 60 miles northeast of Tuba City and 32 miles southwest of Kayenta. Paved roads within the monument go from Tuba City to Kayenta and also connect the headquarters with US 160. The rest of the roads are dirt, making it advisable to check on their condition prior to driving into the monument. Betatakin is reached by paved road 15 miles north of US 164.

Airport

Page Municipal, Las Vegas Sectional
Latitude: 36–55
Longitude: 111–27
FSS: 801-586-3806
Car rentals

Season

The monument is at 7,300 feet and is open year-round, 24 hours a day. During the winter, the entrance road is closed, but the campground is still open.

Climate

Summer days can reach 90° F, but the nights are generally cool. Temperatures in January through March are in the 40s; April and May average 60 to 70; September through December 40s to 70s. Expect brief, hard thunderstorms from June through August.

Accommodations

Holiday Inn: 602-697-3221

In Kayenta:
    Wetherill Inn Motel: 602-697-3231

In Tuba City:
    Van's Trading Post, Tsegi Trading Post, Tsegi AZ.

Camping: A campground is located near headquarters. It has no water during the winter months. No food is available in the park, but some camping supplies are available at trading posts at Black Mesa, 9 miles from the campground, or in Kayenta, 32 miles away.

Features

The Betatakin ruin, "Hillside House," is located in a side canyon of Tsegi Canyon and was built on the floor of a symmetrical cave. This large pueblo originally had 150 rooms and tree rings indicating that it was occupied between 1242 and 1300 A.D. The area has half a dozen ceremonial kivas.

Keet Seel, "Broken Pottery," is the largest and best preserved cliff ruin in Arizona, built between 1240 and 1282 A.D. These dwellings were built in a cave larger than a football field and had over 200 rooms. However, it's the least accessible of all the ruins and is reached on horseback via an 8-mile primitive trail.

Inscription House, the smallest of the three communities, has over 65 rooms. Check to see if visitors are being allowed in. They were working on stabilizing it at last report.

Activities

No visitors are allowed in the ruins unless accompanied by a guide.

You get a good view of Betatakin at Sandal Point, from which you can take a guided tour into the cliff city. Guided tours are conducted daily during the summer at 8:30 A.M. and 1:30 P.M. The tour takes 3 hours, and involves a mile climb gaining 700 feet from the canyon floor to the rim.

To tour Keet Seel, make reservations at Headquarters in Tonalea: 602-672-2366. It's recommended that you join a guided horseback trip to tour this cliff dwelling, leaving at 8:00 A.M. from Memorial Day through Labor Day. Reservations should be made by 4:30 P.M. the preceding day. A daily limit is set on the number of hiking and horse trips permitted.

Hike Sandal Trail, a 1-mile round-trip to the Betatakin Point overlook. Hikers need to obtain permits, which must be picked up by 9:30 A.M. the morning of the hike.

The visitors center has a slide show on the Anasazi, and offers evening campground programs during the summer.

Information

Superintendent
Navajo National Monument
Tonalea, AZ 86044
602-602-2366 or 2367

PIPE SPRING NATIONAL MONUMENT

The monument is located almost at the Utah border, 15 miles southwest of Fredonia, AZ. If you drive from Fredonia, watch for a large steamship rock formation between Fredonia and Spring. It actually looks like an ocean liner sailing through the desert.

Climate

The monument is 1 mile high. The summer days are warm, but the evenings are cool.

Airport

St. George Municipal, Las Vegas Sectional
Latitude: 37–05
Longitude: 113–36
FSS: 801-628-2655

Accommodations

Thunderbird Motor Lodge: 602-673-6123
Rodeway Inn: 602-673-6161
Lamplighter Inn: 602-673-4679

Camping and picnicking are not permitted in the monument.

Features

You can see a well-preserved Mormon fort that was settled by some followers of Brigham Young. One of the buildings was built over the springs, protecting it against Indian attack.

The spring was named in 1858 when members of a Mormon party were sent by Brigham Young to visit with the Indians. One of the members of the group was urged to perform some sharpshooting acts. The sharpshooter challenged one of the members of his party to put his clay pipe on a rock near the spring so that the mouth of the pipe's bowl faced them. He bet he could shoot the bottom of the bowl without touching the pipe's rim. He succeeded.

Activities

Visit "Windsor Castle," a two-story fortlike structure completed in 1871, and located at the base of the red cliffs. The surrounding walls had defensive loopholes with a firing platform located several feet below the top of one of the walls.

From April through September you can watch a living history program in which demonstrations of pioneer life 100 years ago are given.

Information

Park Superintendent
Pipe Spring National Monument
Moccasin, AZ 86022
602-643-5505

SUNSET CRATER NATIONAL MONUMENT

Sunset Crater is 17 miles from Flagstaff via US Highway 89. A hard-surfaced road connects the monument with the Wupatki monument.

Airport

Pulliam, Phoenix Sectional
Latitude: 35–08
Longitude: 111–40
FSS: 800-352-0512
Car rentals:
    Avis: 800-331-1800
    Budget: 800-527-0700

Accommodations

In Flagstaff:
    Best Western Little America, restaurant: 602-779-2741
    Best Western Pony Soldier Motel, restaurant: 602-526-2388
    Comfort Inn, restaurant: 602-774-7326

A campground is located across from the visitors center. It's open around April 1 through November 15.

Features

The area contains many jagged lava flows, cinder cones, including a 1,000-foot cone whose summit is tinted with red and orange, and black volcanic ash that covers hundreds of square miles. The crater's colors look as if the sun were always setting with its dark base and various shades of yellow climbing up the crater walls.

The volcano erupted sometime between 1064 and 1250 A.D., with the lava covering 800 square miles. It was the youngest in the San Francisco Mountains volcanic field, which has over 400 volcanoes. The highest peak is 12,600-foot Humphreys Peak. The last of the eruptions occurred about 900 years ago.

Early settlers moved into the area when they found that the cinder blanket acted as a moisture-retaining mulch, making the land excellent for farming their crops. It's estimated the population once reached 8,000.

One of the largest towns in the area had a population of 300 in the 1200s. They constructed a three-story structure containing 100 rooms.

Activities

A visitors center is located 2 miles from Highway 89.

Hike the Lava Flow Nature Trail at base of the cone, across some of the old lava flows and past a small lava cave. You can also see an ice cave near the foot of the cone. Hiking on the crater is prohibited.

Information

Superintendent
Rt. 3, Box 149
Flagstaff, AZ 86001
602-526-0586

TONTO NATIONAL MONUMENT

The monument is located 1 mile off the highway, 3 miles southeast of Roosevelt or 30 miles northwest of Globe near Roosevelt Lake.

Airports

Scottsdale Municipal, Phoenix Sectional
Latitude: 33–37

Longitude: 111–54
FSS: 602-275-4121
Car rentals:
    Hertz: 602-948-2400

Payson, Phoenix Sectional
Latitude: 34–15
Longitude: 111–20
FSS: 800-352-0512
Car rentals: 602-474-5486

Climate

The monument is open year-round, but the most pleasant weather is during October and June. Summer temperatures are often very high.

Accommodations

The motel and restaurant closest to the monument:
    Lake Roosevelt Resort: 602-467-2276.

In Tonto:
    Punkin Center Lodge: 602-479-2229

In Globe:
    Copper Manor Motel: 602-425-7124
    El Rey Motel: 602-425-4427

In Miami:
    Best Western Copper Hills Inn: 602-425-7151

In Scottsdale:
    Clarion Inn at McCormick Ranch Inn, restaurant, airport transportation, 602-948-7750
    Doubletree Hotel at Scottsdale Mall, restaurant, 602-994-9203
    Marriott's Camelback Inn, restaurant, airport transportation, 602-948-1700

In Payson:
    Bud's Western Lodge Motel: 602-474-2382
    Lazy D Ranch: 602-474-2442
    Diamond Dart Motel: 602-474-2001

Camping: KOA in Payson. Also, a National Forest campground is located along Roosevelt Lake and in nearby Tonto National Forest.

Features

The monument encompasses three major cliff dwellings: Upper Ruin with 40 rooms, Lower Ruins with 19 rooms, and the Lower Ruins Annex, with 13 rooms.

The Salado Indians moved into this basin in 1100 A.D., first living beside the river and then moving into caves in the cliff around 1300 A.D. They were advanced potters and weavers who also traded widely.

Activities

The visitors center contains specimens of one of the best preserved collections of prehistoric fabrics made of vegetable material found anywhere in the Southwest.

Hike up the steep self-guided trail to Lower Ruin, a village of 19 rooms built in a natural cave. Here you can see high walls of quartzite stone laid in mud mortar. The trail closes at 4:00 P.M. daily.

You can enter the 40 rooms of Upper Ruin (Fig. 2) only with a guide and after making prior arrangements. For advance reservations made at least 2 to 3 days early, write the superintendent. Tours begin at 9 A.M. only and accommodate up to 25 visitors. Tours will be cancelled if it's raining. Boots and water are recommended. The hike requires 3 hours and is 3 miles round-trip.

The rangers also conduct 3-hour tours to other less accessible cliff dwellings by reservation only.

While in the monument you can see the Tonto Natural Bridge, located on a rough side road. The bridge arches 183 feet high and is 400 feet long, making it the world's largest travertine arch. It was created by layers of limestone being deposited by the mineral springs one drop at a time. The bridge is privately owned.

Nearby Attractions

Tour the Salt River Canyon, often referred to as the mini-Grand Canyon. The river has exposed more rock layers than you can see in the Grand Canyon. It offers good rock hounding for semiprecious stones and fossils.

There's also good fishing available in the lakes, especially in Seneca Lake, 4 miles south of the Salt River.

Fig. 2. Tonto National Monument. (National Park Service Photo by Richard Frear)

Roosevelt Lake is stocked for fishing, camping, and picnicking. Complete facilities are available at Roosevelt Marina, 1 mile east of the dam.

Information

Superintendent
P.O. Box 707
Roosevelt, AZ 85545
602-467-2241

TUZIGOT NATIONAL MONUMENT

Tuzigot National Monument is 54 miles south on US Highway 89A from Flagstaff, and 2 miles east of Clarkdale.

Airports

Prescott-Ernest A. Love Field, Phoenix Sectional
Latitude: 34–39
Longitude: 112–25

FSS: 602-257-9792 or 800-228-4160
Car rentals

Sedona, Phoenix Sectional
Latitude: 34–52
Longitude: 111–47
FSS: 800-352-0512
Car rentals

Pulliam, Phoenix Sectional
Latitude: 35–08
Longitude: 111–40
FSS: 602-779-3890
Car rentals:
    Avis: 800-331-2221
    Budget: 800-527-0700

Accommodations

In Sedona:
    Best Western Rondee Motor Hotel, restaurant:
        602-282-7131

Sky Ranch Lodge: 602-282-7125
Canyon Portal, restaurant: 602-282-7125
Matterhorn Motor Lodge, restaurant nearby:
602-282-7176

In Prescott:
Buena Vista: 602-445-5660
Best Western Prescottonian Motel, restaurant:
602-445-3096
Comfort Inn, restaurant nearby: 602-778-5770

Features

The monument features an Indian settlement built of old pueblo masonry houses. It's located on top of a long limestone ridge 120 feet above the Verde River.

Tuz is a small 12-room pueblo, typical of ones built in the Verde Valley. At its peak, it was two stories high with 89 ground-floor and 21 second-floor rooms. The rooms averaged 12 by 18 feet. The inhabitants entered the rooms via ladders to the roof, and then came in through ceiling hatchways.

Tuzigot was one of Arizona's principal towns for over three centuries. The people apparently lived here between 1100 and 1450 A.D.

Activities

The visitors center has exhibits of pottery, shell beads, and bracelets.

Information

Park Superintendent
P.O. Box 68
Clarkdale, AZ 86324
602-634-5564

WALNUT CANYON NATIONAL MONUMENT

The monument is located in northern Arizona. You can land in Flagstaff and take I-40, US 66 for 7½ miles, where you meet an oiled highway that goes another 3 miles to the monument.

Airport

Pulliam, Phoenix Sectional
Latitude: 35–08

Longitude: 111–40
FSS: 602-779-3890
Car rentals:
Avis: 800-331-2221
Budget: 800-527-0700

Accommodations

In Flagstaff:
Best Western Little America, restaurant open 24 hours: 602-779-2741
Rodeway Inn, courtesy car: 602-774-5038
Quality Inn, restaurant: 602-774-8771 or 800-774-8771

Features

Walnut Canyon preserves over 300 cliff dwellings, which are an example of the Sinagua culture. There are many small surface ruins that have been weathered into unspectacular mounds of rock and clay.

The major occupation of the area began after the mid-1100s following the eruption of Sunset Crater, continuing through the mid-1200s. At its peak, the population is estimated to have reached around 500. The cliff-dwelling Indians were Stone Age people who had no knowledge of metal and had no domestic animals except dogs and possibly turkeys.

Activities

Besides the cliff dwellings, you can also tour surface features along the rim.

A 1¾-mile round-trip on the self-guided Ruins Trail circles 25 of the best preserved rooms. Caution should be used, as the trail is steep, climbing 185 feet up 240 steps.

You can also follow a ½-mile level trail along the rim to get a good look at two excavated, reconstructed surface dwellings. However, the trail might be closed during the winter because of ice and snow.

Information

Park Superintendent
Rt. 1, Box 25
Flagstaff, AZ 86001
602-526-3367

WUPATKI NATIONAL MONUMENT

The monument is 35 miles north of Flagstaff on US 89. The visitors center is 14 miles from US 89. From there, it's 18 mil ; by paved road south to Sunset Crater National Monument.

Airport

Pulliam, Phoenix Sectional
Latitude: 35–08
Longitude: 111–40
FSS: 602-779-3890
Car rentals:
    Avis: 800-331-2221
    Budget: 800-527-0700

Accommodations

In Flagstaff:
    Best Western Little America, restaurant: 602-779-2741
    Best Western Pony Soldier Motel, restaurant: 602-526-2388
    Comfort Inn, restaurant: 602-774-7326

Features

Prior to the volcanic eruption, Indians lived in pit houses, but experienced great difficulty in growing crops because of the lack of moisture. Following the eruption, the volcano spread ash all over the area, which the Indians found formed an excellent mulch for their corn. Soon the area became the site of a prehistoric land rush, causing the population to increase.

During the 1100s, Wupatki, Hopi for "Tall House," became the largest pueblo in the region. It had over 100 rooms, rose three stories, and had a population of 250 to 300 people. These prehistoric pueblos were occupied from 1100 to 1225 A.D.

Activities

You can see The Citadel, an unexcavated apartment house of 50 rooms built along the edge of the lava-capped limestone sinkhole.

Near the town of Wupatki, an open-air amphitheater was built. Below it you can see a stone masonry ceremonial ballcourt.

Information

Superintendent
Wupatki-Sunset Crater National Monument
Tuba Star Route
Flagstaff, AZ 86001
602-774-7000

Pea Ridge National Military Park

Arkansas

PEA RIDGE NATIONAL MILITARY PARK

The park is 10 miles northeast of Rogers in northwestern Arkansas.

Airport

Rogers Municipal-Carter Field
Kansas City Sectional
Latitude: 36–22
Longitude: 94–06
FSS: 800-482-1159
Car rentals

Accommodations

Town and Country Motor Inn, restaurant:
   501-636-3820
Hiway Host Inn, restaurant: 501-636-9600
Jan-Lin Motor Inn, restaurant: 501-636-1733

Camping: KOA, and Corps of Engineers Beaver Lake Project.

Features

The Civil War Battle of Pea Ridge is also referred to as the Battle of Elkhorn Tavern. It was fought on March 7 and 8, 1862, and resulted in securing Missouri for the Union.

Old Telegraph Road is over 150 years old, and once served as part of the Butterfield Overland routes.

Activities

The visitors center has a slide show and exhibits. A self-guided tour of the battlefield starts there.

You can also hike along a 10-mile Boy Scout Trail and a ½-mile nature trail. Bicyclists can cycle 7 miles along the tour road.

Information

Superintendent
Pea Ridge National Military Park
Pea Ridge, AR 72751
501-451-8122

Golden Gate National Recreation Area

Death Valley National Monument

Cabrillo National Monument

California

CABRILLO NATIONAL MONUMENT

The monument is located 10 miles west on Catalina Blvd, CA 209, on the tip of Point Loma, north of San Diego. Approach the monument through the gates of the Naval Ocean Systems Center in Cabrillo Memorial Park.

Airport

San Diego-Brown Field Municipal
Los Angeles Sectional
Latitude: 32–34
Longitude: 116–58
FSS: 619-291-6381 or 800-532-3815
Car rentals

Season and Climate

Open year-round 9:00 A.M. to 5:15 P.M. Highs in December-May are in the 60s with lows in the 50s. June to November, highs are in the 70s with lows in the 50s.

Accommodations

San Diego has too many to list, and they should be no problem to locate.

In Pt. Loma/Shelter Island:
Cabrillo Motor Lodge: 619-223-5544 (collect calls accepted)
Best Western Shelter Island Marina Inn: 800-351-5500 (In California)
Half Moon Inn: 800-854-2900

In California: 800-532-3737

Camping: San Diego KOA; Cuyamaca Rancho State Park, Anza Borrego Desert State Park, Dixon Lake or Cleveland National Forest. To rent an RV, call 619-447-2639.
You can also camp on one of the state beaches: South Carlsbad and San Elijo. Summer reservations are encouraged and can be made through Ticketron.

Features

In 1542, Portuguese explorer-navigator Juan Rodriguez Cabrillo explored the entire length of the California coast.
The old lighthouse serves as a vantage point for observing the annual migration of gray whales from December through mid-February. It's furnished as it was when it was built in 1855.

Activities

While you're en route to the monument, stop along the ocean by Point Loma to see Sunset Cliffs, where the water has carved some fantastic shapes. The tidepools here are also fascinating.

The monument has a visitors center and museum, and a hike along the Bayside Trail.

From December through February, visit the monument overlook to observe the annual migration of the gray whales.

Take a morning balloon flight over the San Diego coastline, followed by a champagne brunch: 619-481-6225. A sunset flight is also fun: 714-672-1388.

San Diego is close to Tijuana, where you can enjoy shopping or attend a Sunday afternoon bullfight May to September. Also watch jai alai, the world's fastest game, nightly except Thursday: 714-282-3636. If you don't want to drive across the border, you can fly into Tijuana International Airport.

The San Diego zoo is world-famous.

Information

Superintendent
Cabrillo National Monument
P.O. Box 6670
San Diego, CA 92106
714-293-5450

DEATH VALLEY NATIONAL MONUMENT

The park is located in the southeast part of California.

Airport

Death Valley National Monument
Las Vegas Sectional
Latitude: 36–28
Longitude: 116–52
FSS: 800-634-6474

The airport is located a short distance from Furnace Creek. 100 low-lead fuel is available, but you'll need to contact the nearby gas station from 8:00 A.M. to 11:00 A.M. or from 2:00 to 5:00 P.M. at 786-2345 (ext. 5) or 786-2343. For ground transportation from the airport, call 714-786-2345.

Stovepipe Wells, Las Vegas Sectional
Latitude: 36–36
Longitude: 17–09
FSS: 800-634-6474
No fuel or rental cars available.

Because there aren't rental cars available at Death Valley, you are somewhat limited in your ground transportation unless you either bring along your own bicycle in your plane, or rent one from the resort. You can take a bus tour to Scotty's Castle.

You may prefer flying into Las Vegas or some other closer area where rental cars are available, and then driving into the area.

Season

The monument is open all year, but it's best from October 15 to May. The area becomes very busy on Washington's Birthday, Easter week, Thanksgiving, Christmas, and during the Death Valley Encampment in early November. Most visitors prefer visiting the area sometime between late November through late April.

Climate

The area is one of the hottest places in the world. Daytime temperatures in the summer can reach as high as 124° F. Air temperatures of 134° F have been recorded, with some ground level temperatures during the summer recorded as high as 190° F. Winter is the best time to visit, since temperatures are more moderate.

The valley only averages 1½ inches of rainfall a year.

Accommodations

Furnace Creek Inn and Ranch: 800-227-4700. Reservations are recommended if you plan to visit during any of the winter holidays.

Stove Pipe Wells Hotel, located near the sand dunes. For reservations, call the operator and ask for Stove Pipe Wells #1.

There are campgrounds near Furnace Creek and Stove Pipe Wells.

Features

The area got its name from the Bennett-Arcane Forty-Niners who were on their way to the California goldfields. They became trapped in the valley as they tried to escape to the south. Some of the miners lost their lives here, and as the rest managed to leave the valley, they looked behind and gave it the name of Death Valley.

The valley's lowest point is at Badwater, 282 feet below sea level. Badwater reportedly is the hottest place on Earth, where a temperature reading of 134° F has been recorded.

Ubehebe Crater is located 8 miles from Scotty's Castle. You can get some good views of the crater from the air.

Racetrack is a 3,708-foot-high dry lake located southwest of the crater. Stones weighing as much as 39 pounds move across the clay floor, leaving their trails behind.

The Devil's Golf Course has many crystalline salt pinnacles and gravels stretching 10 miles across the valley floor. Try to be there when one of the naturalists lectures.

Scotty's Castle was built by Johnson, a wealthy Chicago insurance executive, to be shared with his wife and one of his closest friends, Walter Scott, a former trick rider for Buffalo Bill's Wild West Show.

Death Valley was also the site of miners who came searching for silver who left their burros behind. These animals are now in the process of being relocated elsewhere.

In 1880, a couple discovered borax, useful in making pottery. You can still see the ruins of the old Harmony Borax Works 2 miles north of Furnace Creek.

Activities

Hikers will find Zabriskie Point in Golden Canyon an interesting spot to explore.

In Titus Canyon you can walk the canyon's 3-mile lower gorge. Also hike for 1½ miles in Grotto Canyon through the water-polished narrows.

If you fly to Stovepipe Wells, you can hike up Mosaic Canyon to see the polished marble narrows.

Hikers can also explore the sand dunes, east of Stovepipe Wells, or hike around Ubehebe Crater.

Mountain climbers can go up Telescope Peak, 11,049 feet high, starting from Mahogany Flat Campground at the head of Wildrose Canyon, or climb 4 miles up to Wildrose Peak's summit: 9,064 feet.

Additional hikes are described in the Park Service's booklet, *Getting Around in the Death Valley Backcountry.*

Bicyclists might enjoy a challenging ride around Artist's Point, 12 miles from Furnace Creek. The road is steep and sandy in many places, but gives you a great view of some of the most colorful rock formations you've ever seen.

Tour Scotty's Castle from 9:00 A.M. to 5:00 P.M. The grounds are open 7:00 A.M. to 7:00 P.M. Tours are conducted on the hour. Admission is charged.

Information

Superintendent
Death Valley National Monument
Death Valley, CA 92328
619-786-2331

GOLDEN GATE
NATIONAL RECREATION AREA

The area is in San Francisco and follows the city's northern and western shoreline. The park is across from the Golden Gate Bridge in Marin County off Highway 101. Follow either Alexander Avenue, Shoreline Highway, or Sir Francis Drake Blvd (Fig. 3).

Airport

San Francisco International, San Francisco Sectional
Latitude: 37–37
Longitude: 122–22
FSS: 800-345-4546

Fig. 3. Marina Headlands with Golden Gate Bridge and San Francisco in background, Golden Gate National Recreation Area. (National Park Service Photo by Richard Frear)

Rental cars, courtesy cars, taxis and public transportation are available from here:

Hertz: 800-654-3131

Avis: 800-331-1800

You can also get to the area via the Municipal Railway bus system, or ride MUNI from downtown San Francisco to the shoreline.

Climate

Wind and fog are common from June to September, especially around Golden Gate. The best time to visit is during the fall, when it's the warmest. The area receives its greatest rainfall from November to April.

Activities

Six historic ships are docked at Hyde Street Pier. You can board three of them. Both self-guided and regular guided tours are available. Ships are open from 10:00 A.M. to 5:00 P.M. For information, call 555-6435.

You can also board the *Balclutha*, a square-rigged sailing ship docked at Pier 43. Hours: 9:00 A.M. to 6:00 P.M. Information: 415-982-1886. You can also see *Jeremiah O'Brien*, a World War II liberty ship docked at Pier 3. For information, call 415-556-0560 or 415-441-3101.

Visit Baker Beach, where you can see a 95,000-pound cannon built in 1904. Weekend tours are provided from 7:00 A.M. to 9:00 P.M. Information: 556-8371.

Visit Aquatic Park, where "hardy" swimmers and fishermen can enjoy themselves. Lifeguards are on duty from April 15 through October 15. Information: 415-566-2904.

Golden Gate Promenade begins here, and you can take a 3½-mile hike following the shoreline to Fort Point National Historic Site to see an example of the brick forts built by the U.S. Army engineers in 1861. It's open 10:00 A.M. to 5:00 P.M. Half-hour tours are conducted on the half hour and hour. Watch the loading and firing of the Civil War cannons daily at 12:30, 2:30, and 3:30 P.M. Information: 415-556-1693.

China Beach has a good swimming beach with lifeguards on duty during the summer; open 7:00 A.M. until dusk. Ocean Beach has a 4 mile shoreline that's good for hiking and jogging.

Hike the Coastal Trail and use MUNI 18 to return to your starting point.

Take a ferry to Alcatraz for a guided tour. The tour requires 2 hours. Reservations: 415-495-4089. For information: 415-555-0560.

Nearby Attractions

Golden Gate Park. To get there from anywhere in the city, call 415-673-6864. Parking is scarce on nice days. Try Lincoln Way or Fulton Street and walk into the park. The east end of Kennedy Drive is closed to cars on Sundays.

The east end of the park is geared to touring on foot, while a bicycle is the best way to see the west end. You can rent bikes along Stanyan Street. You can also go for a ride in a horse-drawn carriage. Tours begin outside the Japanese Tea Garden.

Free guided tours are offered on weekends from May to October. For information, call 415-221-1311.

When the weather is good, attend a Sunday band concert at the Temple of Music bandshell in the Music Concourse at 1:00 P.M. For information, call 415-558-4268.

Stop in at the Japanese Tea Garden for tea and rice cakes. Guided tours of the nearby gardens are offered Sunday afternoons May through October.

Visit Tennessee Valley, where you can hike a 2-mile trail to a small beach and a hike-in campground. Sites are available by reservation only. For information, call 415-383-7717. For campground reservations, call 415-331-1540.

Visit Muir Beach and Stinson Beach. You can only swim on Stinson Beach from late May through mid-September when it's guarded. Information: 415-868-0942. Weather: 415-868-1922.

Angel Island State Park has a 5-mile trail around the island. Information: 415-435-1915.

Olema Valley is billed as a hiker's paradise. The trails here are long and often steep. Information: 415-663-1092.

Drive around 17-Mile Drive on the Monterrey Peninsula Toll Road located in the Del Monte Forest. You pass Pebble Beach Golf Links.

Stop at Point Lobos Preserve to see the Monterrey cypress. The preserve was the first underwater preserve in the nation. You can do some limited diving in two coves.

Information

Superintendent
Golden Gate National Recreation Area
Ft. Mason
San Francisco, CA 94123
415-556-0560

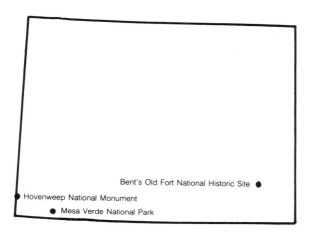

Bent's Old Fort National Historic Site ●
● Hovenweep National Monument
● Mesa Verde National Park

Colorado

BENT'S OLD FORT
NATIONAL HISTORIC SITE

The fort is 8 miles east of La Junta and 15 miles from Las Animas.

Airports

La Junta Municipal, Wichita Sectional
Latitude: 38–03
Longitude: 103–31
FSS: 303-384-4311
Car rentals

City and County of Las Animas, Wichita Sectional
Latitude: 38–03
Longitude: 103–14
FSS: 303-384-4311
Taxi

Accommodations

In La Junta:
    Kit Carson Hotel: 303-384-4471
    Stagecoach Motor Inn: 303-384-5476
    La Junta TraveLodge: 303-384-2504

In Las Animas:
    Sunset Motel: 303-456-0551

Features

The fort was once the hub for American trade going south to Mexico, west into the Great Basin, and north to Wyoming.

Indians also brought goods to trade here, along with the mountain men who traded their beaver pelts for supplies. William Bent was instrumental in establishing peaceful relations between the rival Indian tribes, who were encouraged to meet and trade at his fort in peace.

Indian warfare in 1847 led to a business decline, and by 1849 the fort no longer was in operation.

Today, the fort has been reconstructed to its 1845-46 appearance.

Activities

Tour the reconstructed fort and watch living history demonstrations.

Watch the famous Koshare Indian Dancers perform dances Saturday at 8:15 from mid-June through mid-August. Information: 303-384-4801, or Chamber of Commerce: 303-384-7411. Look through the kiva to see their art, beadwork, and pottery.

Information

Superintendent
Bent's Old Fort National Historic Site
35110 Highway 194E
La Junta, CO 81050-9523
303-384-2596

HOVENWEEP NATIONAL MONUMENT

The momument is located 45 miles west of Cortez. Roads leading into the monument are graded dirt, so be sure to check on their conditions before entering the monument, particularly during inclement weather.

Airport

Cortez-Montezuma County, Denver Sectional
Latitude: 37–18
Longitude: 108–38
FSS: 303-565-3023
Car rentals: Hertz: 800-654-3131
There is bus service into Mesa Verde from Cortez. It runs from 7:00 A.M. until 4:30 P.M. daily. Contact Ara Mesa Verde Company: 303-533-7731.

Climate

The best time to visit is spring or fall, when the daytime temperatures range from the 50s to the 70s. Winter temperatures range in the 30s and 40s and summer daytime temperatures are in the 90s.

Accommodations

No food, lodging, service stations, or paved roads are available in the monument.

In Cortez:
Bel Rau Lodge: 303-565-3738
Turquoise Motor Inn, restaurant: 303-565-3475
Best Western Sands: 303-565-3761

A campground is available with water, but no wood. The closest supplies are at Ismay Trading Post, 14 miles southeast.

Features

The monument was established to preserve several groups of prehistoric Pueblo Indian ruins.

The ruin sites in Colorado include Cutthroat Castle, Hackberry Ruin, Horseshoe Ruin, and Holly Ruin. Square Tower and Cajon Ruins are in Utah, where the monument headquarters is located.

Access roads to other ruins are unmarked and generally require the use of four-wheel-drive. All ruins except Square Tower, the largest and best preserved, are isolated and difficult to reach.

Activities

You can follow a self-guided trail through the Square Tower group ruins. A park ranger is on duty year-round there. A 4-mile trail leaves Square Tower Group and goes to Holly Ruin.

Information

Superintendent
Mesa Verde National Park, CO 81330
303-529-4461

Hovenweep National Monument
McElmo Rt
Cortez, CO 81331

MESA VERDE NATIONAL PARK

Mesa Verde, ''Green Table'' in Spanish, is located in southwestern Colorado off Highway 160 between Cortez and Mancos.

Airports

Cortez-Montezuma County, Denver Sectional
Latitude: 37–18
Longitude: 108–38
FSS: 303-565-3023
Car rentals: Hertz: 800-654-3131
There is bus service into Mesa Verde from Cortez. It runs from 7:00 A.M. until 4:30 P.M. daily. Contact Ara Mesa Verde Company: 533-7731.

Durango-La Plata County, Denver Sectional
Latitude: 37–09
Longitude: 107–45
FSS: 303-247-3116
Car rentals and Gray Line bus: 303-259-0090; runs daily May through September.

Season and Climate

The park is open year-round, and the best time to visit is early May through October 15, since this is the only time lodging, meals, groceries, and gas are available.

Temperatures near park headquarters range from an average low of 18° F in January to a high of 88° F in July. Extremes of −20° F and 102° F have been recorded. Summer days range from 85° to 100° F with evenings 55 to 65. Spring daytime temperatures are between 50° and 70° F. Fall days are in the 50s and 60s.

For current road conditions call 303-529-4475 or 303-529-4461.

Accommodations

No food or lodging is available in the park from mid-October through mid-April.

In the park:
> Far View Motel. Reservations: 303-529-4421
> from May 15-October 15
> Call 303-533-7731 the rest of the year.

In Mancos, approximately 28 miles from park headquarters:
> Echo Basin Ranch: 303-533-7000
> Enchanted Mesa Motel: 303-533-7729
> Mesa Verde Motel: 303-533-7741

In Cortez, approximately 30 miles from park headquarters:
> Aneth Lodge Friendship Inn: 303-565-3453
> El Capri Motel: 303-565-3764
> Ramada Inn: 303-565-3773

In Durango:
> Rodeway Inn: 303-385-4980

Thunderbird Lodge: 303-258-2540
Travel Inn Motel: 303-247-0593

Camping: Double A Campground at the entrance to the park, Mesa Verde Point Kampark, and Morefield Canyon Campground.

Features

Mesa Verde was named for the pinon and juniper that cover its tabletop, 2,000 feet above the valley floor. The park has 20 miles of paved roads, with its highest point reaching 8,572 feet.

The complex (Fig. 4) is considered to be the most notable and best pre-Columbian ruins in the United States. Visitors can see at least three kinds of ruins: pit houses, pueblos, and cliff dwellings, representing the progress of the prehistoric peoples living in the area for over 1,200 years.

Fig. 4. Cliff Palace at Mesa Verde National Park.

The cliff-dwelling Indians came here during the first century A.D. In the sixth century they moved to the mesa tops, where they found a plentiful supply of water and began to build their permanent rock shelters.

The cities of Mesa Verde were occupied for almost 800 years, and abandoned at the end of the thirteenth century. The largest of the cities are believed to have housed 400 people, with communities of 2,000 to 4,000 people.

Spruce Tree House's high walls still touch the top of the cave. The original roofs are still intact. It had 114 rooms and 8 *kivas*, which were underground ceremonial chambers for men only.

Cliff Palace is the largest and most famous of the ruins, and was built under a high, vaulted cave roof. It has more than 200 rooms, of which 23 are kivas. Tourists squeeze through small openings and climb two 18-foot ladders when touring this palace.

Balcony House has 40 rooms that show the architectural detail and construction skills of the inhabitants. It is reached by crawling through a 12-foot tunnel that could easily be defended by one man.

Activities

The mesa is only accessible during the summer via public transportation. The bus leaves Far View Visitors Center parking lot every half hour from 9:00 A.M. to 3:00 P.M.. You see two ruins, Step House and Long House, where guided tours are offered. Step House is on a self-guided basis.

Ruins Road begins ½ mile north of the museum and has two 6-mile self-guided loops open from 8:00 A.M. until sunset.

Balcony House may only be toured in the company of a ranger every half hour daily 9:00 A.M. to 5:00 P.M., from Memorial Day through Labor Day. This tour involves climbing a 30-foot ladder and crawling through the original access tunnel.

You can take a self-guided tour of Spruce Tree House during the summer months from May through September from 8:30 A.M. to 6:30 P.M. Ranger-guided tours are offered at Spruce Tree House three times daily during the winter.

Cliff Palace is the largest and most scenic ruin in the park. It can be seen from Mesa Top Drive across Cliff Canyon. Then, if you want to hike down to the ruin, it takes approximately 10 minutes for a summer self-guided tour available daily from 9:00 A.M. to 6:30 P.M. A Park Service ranger is on duty during the spring and fall, depending upon the weather and trail conditions.

Far View Ruins are also toured on a self-guided basis, and are visited during the winter by cross-country skiers. The ruins are open from 8:00 A.M. until sunset from mid-April through mid-November.

Hiking trails include Spruce Canyon Trail, which drops off Chapin Mesa and goes to the bottom of the canyon.

Petroglyph Point Trail, a 2.8-mile hike, begins at the park headquarters and winds along the base of Cliff House.

Prater Ridge Trail begins on a hill west of Morefield Campground and makes a 7½ mile loop around the cliffs of the ridge.

Bikers can enjoy cycling along the ruins road. The road is open daily from 8:00 A.M. until sunset from March 16 to December 14, depending upon the weather conditions.

Information

Superintendent
Mesa Verde National Park, CO 81330
303-529-4465

Nearby Features

Lowry Pueblo Ruins is reached by driving out US 666 to Pleasant View and then west on County Road CC for 9 miles. Take a self-guided tour. Open daily from 8:30 A.M. to dusk. For information: Cortez Chamber of Commerce: 303-565-3414.

Ute Mountain Tribal Park is reached by following US 666 for 15 miles south of Cortez. Take a day-long tour of some Anasazi ruins. Advance reservations are necessary from May through August.

Information

Ute Mountain Tribal Park
Towaoc, CO 81334
303-565-3751

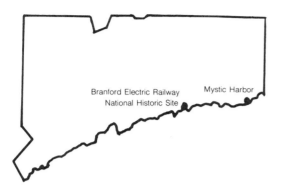

Branford Electric Railway
National Historic Site

Mystic Harbor

Connecticut

BRANFORD ELECTRIC RAILWAY NATIONAL HISTORIC SITE

The railway is east of New Haven at the foot of River Street.

Airport

Tweed-New Haven, New York Sectional
Latitude: 41–16
Longitude: 72–53
FSS: 800-972-2271
Car rentals:
    Avis: 203-624-2161
    Hertz: 203-777-6861
    Budget: 203-787-1143

Accommodations

Howard Johnson's Lodge, restaurant:
    203-562-1111
Holiday Inn at Yale, restaurant: 203-777-6221
Colony Inn, restaurant: 203-776-1234

Activities

Take a 3-mile ride aboard one of the early 1900s trolley cars. On your return trip, you'll stop by the carbarn and restoration area to see over 100 trolley cars in various states of reconstruction. Hours: 11:00 A.M. to 5:00 P.M. daily. Cars operate every 30 minutes, but more frequently if necessary.

A National Trolley Festival is held Saturday and Sunday during the first weekend in June. Watch a parade of various trolley cars and take rides between shows, which begin at 12:00, 2:30, and 4:30 P.M..

Nearby Attractions

In 1716, Yale University was moved to New Haven, and has many beautiful ivy-covered buildings. Free guided tours begin at Phelps Archway, 344 College. For information, call 203-436-8330.

Take a Liberty Belle cruise from Long Wharf Dock. Call 203-562-4163.

MYSTIC HARBOR

The harbor is in eastern Connecticut along Long Island Sound.

Airport

Groton/New London, New York Sectional
Latitude: 41–19

Longitude: 72–03
FSS: 203-445-8549 or 800-972-2271
Car rentals

Accomodations

Groton Motor Inn: 203-445-9784
Holiday Inn: 203-445-8141
Quality Inn: 203-445-8141
Thomas Botel and Harbour Inn: 203-445-8111

Features

Mystic Harbor is where the fastest clipper ships in the country were built during the middle of the nineteenth century. The shipyards were also responsible for the building of the first regular ironclad vessel, the *Galena*, which was constructed in 1861 (Fig. 5).

The harbor was also the site for the building of the last of the nineteenth century whaling ships, the *Charles W. Morgan*, the *Joseph Conrad*, and other vessels now on exhibit at the wharves along the waterfront.

Activities

Visit Olde Mistick Village, a shopping complex that has 25 colonial-style buildings. The village has a handcrafted water wheel and a community meeting house where you can view an orientation film.

A walk through some of the shops will give you a good idea of the crafts done by the early seaport inhabitants. Watch demonstrations on shipbuilding and ship rigging. Other buildings have ship models, scrimshaw, figureheads, and old logbooks.

Visit the Mystic Marinelife Aquarium, which features more than 2,000 specimens.

A mile and a half from town, visit the Denison Homestead to see a well-preserved example of early eighteenth-century architecture. Now it's become a museum of home life in New England from early colonial times until the 1900s. Information: 203-536-9248.

Another restored mansion is the Whitehall Mansion. This building is a pre-Revolutionary home with colonial furnishings. It's open Monday through Friday and Sunday from 2 to 4, May 1st to October 15th.

Nearby Attraction

Just beyond Mystic, the U.S.S. *Nautilus* is permanently moored and is now open for tours. The *Nautilus* is the world's first nuclear-powered vessel and the adjoining museum has a good historical display of submarines from Bushnell's Turtle to the more modern class subs, the *Los Angeles* and *Ohio*.

Fig. 5. Mystic Harbor offers the opportunity to see several historic ships.

Ft. Delaware
State Park ●

Delaware

FORT DELAWARE STATE PARK

The park is on Pea Patch Island between New Castle and Delaware City.

Airport

Greater Wilmington-New Castle County,
Washington Sectional
Latitude: 39–41
Longitude: 75–36
FSS: 609-825-1173

Accommodations

In New Castle:
    Quality Inn Skyways, restaurant: 302-328-6666
    El Rancho Motel, restaurant: 302-328-7377

Quality Inn, restaurant open 24 hours:
    302-328-6246

Season

The fort is only open weekends and holidays from late April through September.

Features

The fort was built in 1859 and was used as a federal prison during the Civil War. It's also a nesting site for egrets, herons, and ibis.

Activities

The fort is accessible only by boat, which leaves the dock at the foot of Clinton Street on Saturdays, Sundays and holidays between 11:00 A.M. and 6:00 P.M. For information, call 302-834-7941.

Charter a fishing boat at the Delaware City Marina: 834-4172.

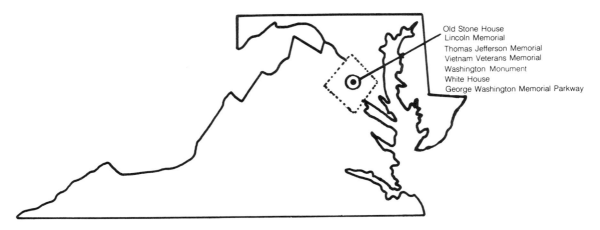

Old Stone House
Lincoln Memorial
Thomas Jefferson Memorial
Vietnam Veterans Memorial
Washington Monument
White House
George Washington Memorial Parkway

District of Columbia

Airports

Dulles International, Washington Sectional
Latitude: 38–56
Longitude: 77–27
FSS: 703-661-8526.
Car rentals
　　You can also ride the Washington Flyer Express Ground Transportation Service into the downtown area. Information: 703-685-1400 or 800-431-5472.

Washington National, Washington Sectional
Latitude: 38–51
Longitude: 77–02
FSS: 703-486-3990
Car rentals
Ground transportation:
　　Airport Motel Commuter Limo: 301-859-3000, or in Washington: 202-261-1091.

Accommodations

Radisson Mark Plaza Hotel: 703-845-1010
Marriott-Crystal Gateway Hotel, airport transportation, restaurant: 703-920-3230
Econo Lodge: 703-832-3200

Comfort Inn: 703-922-9200 or 800-228-5150
Loews L'Enfant Hotel (near the mall), four restaurants with others in underground plaza: 202-484-1000.
Hyatt Regency (Capitol Hill): 202-737-1234
Also contact Washington Central Reservations: 800-554-2200 or 703-289-2220

Access

　　Access to the memorials is via tourmobile, which stops 18 times along the Mall, at West Potomac Park, and at Arlington. Your boarding pass is good all day. For information, call 202-638-5371 or 202-554-7950.
　　A separate tour begins at Arlington National Cemetery's visitors center, where tours of the cemetery, Arlington House, and stops at the Kennedy gravesites are offered. Changing of the guard at the Tomb of the Unknown Soldier occurs every half hour during the summer. You can also arrange tours of Mt. Vernon and Cedar Hill here.

Climate

　　Summers can be hot and humid. Fall features warm days with cool nights. Winters can be very cold. Cherry blossom season is usually in late March through early April.

THOMAS JEFFERSON MEMORIAL

Jefferson, at the age of 33, was elected to be a delegate to the Continental Congress and was chosen to draft the Declaration of Independence. He served as vice president for John Adams, and then served two terms as United States president in 1801.

"I have sworn upon the altar of God eternal hostility against every form of tyranny over the mind of man." This and other famous quotes of Jefferson are inscribed inside his memorial, which also contains a bronze statue by Rudolph Evans.

The memorial (Fig. 6) is best seen around the first two weeks of April when the cherry trees are in bloom. Attend the Annual Cherry Blossom Festival staged near the Tidal Basin.

Talks are given every 30 minutes. Information: 202-426-6841.

LINCOLN MEMORIAL

The memorial was designed by Henry Bacon and sculpted by Daniel Chester French. It has 36 columns to symbolize each state in the Union during Lincoln's lifetime. Near the statue is a copy of his Gettysburg Address and his second inaugural address.

The memorial is made of white Colorado yule marble. If you look on the attic walls, you can see the names of the 48 states that were part of the Union in 1922, along with their admission dates. Alaska

Fig. 6. Jefferson Memorial.

and Hawaii's names were added by an inscription on the terrace leading to the memorial. Half-hour tours are offered.

OLD STONE HOUSE

The Old Stone House is located at 3051 M Street, NW, in Georgetown. It's believed to be the only surviving pre-Revolutionary building in Washington. It was built in 1765.

To tour the house, pick up a pamphlet from the Park Service. A description is included in the self-guided walking tour guide for Georgetown. It's open Wednesday through Sunday, and is closed holidays.

Hikers and bikers have access to the nearby C&O Canal towpath located a block from the house on the Foundry Mall, 1055 Thomas Jefferson St. NW. A mule-drawn barge goes to Great Falls Wednesday-Sunday. The Barge goes to Great Falls Tavern, Maryland, and returns. For reservations and information: 202-472-4376.

VIETNAM VETERANS' MEMORIAL

The memorial was designed as a symbol to the 58,000 men and women who died or who were reported missing in the war, the longest in our nation's history. It's in the Constitution Gardens near the Lincoln Memorial (Fig. 7).

The U.S. Marine Corps War Memorial is nearby and features 32-foot figures with faces of the men who did the actual flag raising on Iwo Jima. Also near here is the Netherlands Carillon. Concerts are presented from 2:00 to 4:00 P.M. Saturdays and on national holidays from April through September. Visitors are invited to go into the tower to watch the carillonneur perform.

The U.S. Marine Corps presents the Marine sunset review parade Tuesday from 7:00 to 8:30 P.M. from June to August. From June to August, attend free outdoor concerts presented by military bands at 8:00 P.M. For information, call 202-433-6060.

WASHINGTON MONUMENT

Washington was honored for his leadership in both the French and Indian War and in the American

Fig. 7. Vietnam Veterans Memorial.

the tour between 8:00 and 10:00 A.M. For information, call 202-456-7041.

GEORGE WASHINGTON MEMORIAL PARKWAY

The parkway connects historic sites including Washington's Mt. Vernon Estate, passes Theodore Roosevelt Island, and provides access to Clara Barton National Historic Site in Maryland. The north end is at Great Falls Park, which is part of the Chesapeake and Ohio Canal National Historic Park. Watch for the mule-drawn barge which turns around here to return to Georgetown.

To take this 1½-hour barge trip, go to the Georgetown Visitors Center at the landing between Thomas Jefferson Street and 30th. Information: 301-299-2026.

Boating is also available along the Potomac River. Contact the National Weather Service at 301-899-3210 for a message about flood stages and hazards along the river. The National Park Service can suggest good spots to put in. One visitors center is in Georgetown and another is at Great Falls.

Bike or run along the 17-mile trail from Mt. Vernon to the Lincoln Memorial.

Additional Attractions

The JFK Center for the Performing Arts has three theaters: Eisenhower Theater, Opera House, and Concert Hall. Tour the Hall of States to see a display of the flags of the United States and its territories in the order in which they entered the Union. Free tours are offered from 10:00 A.M. to 1:15 P.M. Tickets may be obtained through Instant-charge: 202-857-0900 or 800-424-8504.

Ford's Theater offers theater performances as well as short presentations on the story of the Lincoln assassination. Information: 202-347-4833.

Rock Creek Park offers visitors the opportunity for hiking trails ranging in length from 3⁷⁄₁₀ miles along the Glover-Archibold Trail to covering 5⅕ miles on the Valley Trail. You can also bike from here into Maryland. Rental bikes, canoes, and rowboats are available at Thompson's Boat House in the park.

Revolution. Following the Revolution, he was chosen to preside over the Constitutional Convention in 1787, and 2 years later was elected as our first president.

The marble came from Maryland, and if you look closely you can see where the shaft was continued in 1880. Even though the marble came from the same quarry, it was from a different strata.

You can reach an observation deck by elevator. Interior walls contain 188 stones presented by various states and nations of the world.

While here, make personal reservations at the booth to tour Mt. Vernon and Cedar Hill. Information: 202-554-5100.

WHITE HOUSE

Tour the White House, whose cornerstone was laid in 1792. It's open to the public from 10:00 A.M. to noon Tuesday through Saturday. Tickets must be picked up in person by everyone wishing to make

Bicyclists wishing to rent bicycles for cycling along the Mt. Vernon Bike Trail may also obtain bikes at the Bicycle Exchange in Alexandria, VA, 768-3444; Big Wheel Bikes, Georgetown, 202-337-0254; and Metropolis Bike and Scooter in DC, 202-543-8900.

The Bureau of Engraving and Printing offers tours every 25 minutes Monday to Friday from 9:00 A.M. to 2:00 P.M. Go early in the morning during tourist season, March through September. For information, call 202-447-9709.

Guided tours are offered through the Capitol Building every 15 minutes 9:00 A.M. to 3:15 P.M. daily. To attend sessions in either the House or Senate, obtain a gallery pass from your congressman or senator. For information, call 202-224-3121.

The Library of Congress is the largest library in the world, established in 1800. Tours are Monday through Saturday 9:00 A.M. to 5:30 P.M., and Sunday 9:00 A.M. to 9:00 P.M. The building's architecture is well worth seeing. For information, call 202-287-5000.

Pilots will particularly enjoy touring the National Air and Space Museum, part of the Smithsonian Institution. Many outstanding exhibits and original aircraft are displayed here, along with good movies. Guided tours are available.

Pilots will also enjoy visiting the Paul E. Gerber Restoration Facility in Suitland, MD. This is the site of air and space restorations for the museum. Tours are available by appointment only. Call Tuesday to Thursday between 10:00 A.M. and 3:00 P.M. for 3-hour tours: 357-1400. Tours go Monday to Friday at 10:00 A.M., and at 10:00 A.M. and 1:00 P.M. on Saturday and Sunday. For information, call 202-357-2700.

Theodore Roosevelt Island, located on the Potomac River, offers a 2½-mile hiking trail. A pedestrian bridge connects the island to the Virginia shore. Information is available at 202-426-6922 or 703-285-2598.

Visit the home of Frederick Douglass in Cedar Hill. Douglass was a former slave who became an advocate of women's rights and was very prominent in the abolition movement. For information, call 202-426-5960.

Information

Superintendent
Rock Creek Park
5000 Glover Rd., NW
Washington, DC 20015-1098

Dial an event for monthly listing of events: 202-737-8866
Dial a Park-NPS activities: 202-426-6975
Dial a Museum (Smithsonian): 202-357-2020
Dial a Ticket (Half price tickets day of show): 202-842-5387

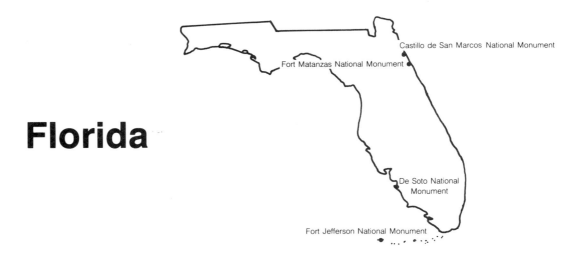

Florida

CASTILLO DE SAN MARCOS NATIONAL MONUMENT

The monument is in St. Augustine.

Airport

St. Augustine Municipal, Jacksonville Sectional
Latitude: 29–57
Longitude: 81–20
FSS: 800-342-1432 or 904-824-9595
Car rentals:
Avis: 904-829-3700

Climate

During the winter months, Florida has little frontal activity with morning fog common on the northern part of the state. Its average rainfall is 50 inches, with temperatures in the 60s to 80s. The state has fewer hurricanes that most other coastal states.

Accommodations

Scottish Inn: 904-829-5543
Monterey Motel: 904-824-4482

Whetstone's Bayfront Inn: 904-824-1681
Bed and Breakfast: Kenwood Inn: 904-824-2116

Camping: North Beach Camp Resort, Ocean Grove, Beachcombers Resort, and St. Augustine KOA.

Features

Castillo de San Marcos is the site of a short-lived colony of France located at Fort Caroline. Castillo was begun in 1672, and required 25 years to complete. It was built of coquina quarried from nearby Anastasia Island, and is the oldest masonry fortification in the United States. The fort was never taken by force, but changed hands four different times through treaty (Fig. 10-1).

During the mid-1800s, the fort was used as a military prison.

Activities

Tour the fort. The cannon is fired on Saturdays, Sundays, and holidays.

Stop by the visitors center and see ''The St. Augustine Adventure.'' The Museum Theater has two movies: *Dream of an Empire* and *Struggle to Survive*.

St. Augustine is the oldest permanent European settlement in the continental United States. It was founded in 1565 by the Spanish.

Some of the historic sights to see include the Cathedral of St. Augustine, built in the 1790s; Doctor Peck's House, which was constructed in the 1690s; the oldest store museum, which has over 100,000 items from life at the turn of the century; and the oldest wooden schoolhouse, which is the oldest wooden structure in the city, built prior to 1763 (Fig. 8).

The Lightner Museum is three blocks long, and houses "Victorian Village." It was formerly the 300-room Alczar Hotel built in 1888 by Henry Flagler.

You can either take a walking tour on your own, or board a sightseeing train at one of five boarding stations. These trains stop at the various attractions, and pass by every 20 minutes. The complete tour covers 7 miles and 80 sights, and may be boarded as often as you want throughout the day. For information, call 904-829-6545.

Walk down the "Street of the Merchants" to see many interesting shops.

The Fountain of Youth Archeological Park is the site of an old Indian town. In 1513, this is where Ponce de Leon came ashore.

Take a 1¼-hour cruise aboard *Victory II*. For information, call 904-824-1806.

In mid-August, attend Days in Spain Fiesta.

In early December, watch the Christmas parade. Then, later in the month, see the Regatta of Lights, a bayfront parade of boats. The town itself is beautifully lighted during this season.

Nearby Attractions

Fort Matanzas National Monument includes the southern tip of Anastasia Island and the northern part of Rattlesnake Island. It is 14 miles south of St. Augustine.

Matanza means slaughter in Spanish, which is what happened in 1565. Jean Ribaut's 500 shipwrecked men were trapped in the Matanza Inlet. From there Menendez marched them across the inlet 10 at a time, where they were slain. This ended France's first attempt to share in the riches of the New World.

You can take a ferry to the fort. For information, call 904-471-0116. A visitors center is on Anastasia Island.

OTHER FLORIDA MONUMENTS

Fort Jefferson National Monument is 70 miles west of Key West on a cluster of seven coral reefs called the Dry Tortugas. The monument is famous for its bird and marine life and for its legends of pirates and sunken gold. Fort Jefferson was the largest of the nineteenth-century American coastal forts.

Public transportation is available to the monument from Key West by amphibious aircraft. Contact the Key West Chamber of Commerce. The

Fig. 8. This school in St. Augustine's is the oldest wooden structure in the city, built prior to 1763.

monument offers a self-guided walking tour, snorkeling, scuba diving, fishing, and picnicking. It's only open during daylight hours.

De Soto National Monument is on the south shore of the Manatee River west of Bradenton. The Monument was named for Don Hernando de Soto, a conquistador of Spain who landed in Florida in 1539 with 600 warriors and 12 priests. They went up through Georgia and Carolina, crossed the Great Smokies, eventually ending up by the Mississippi River. Here de Soto caught a fever and died. His followers sank his coffin in the river.

The monument has a visitors center and nature trail.

Information

Superintendent
Everglades National Park
P.O. Box 279
Homestead, FL 33030
305-247-6211

Superintendent
De Soto National Monument
75th Street NW
Bradenton, FL 33529
813-792-0458

Georgia

CHICKAMAUGA and CHATTANOOGA NATIONAL MILITARY PARK

The park's largest section is located in Georgia, with some in Tennessee. The visitors center is 9 miles south of Chattanooga on US 27.

Airport

Chattanooga-Lovell, Atlanta Sectional
Latitude: 35–02
Longitude: 85–12
WS: 615-892-6302
Rental cars:
    Avis: 800-331-1800
    Budget: 800-527-0700
    National: 800-328-4567

Accommodations

In Chattanooga:
    Chattanooga Choo-Choo Hilton: 615-266-5000
    Ramada Inn: 615-622-8353
    Rodeway Inn: 615-894-6720

Camping in KOA, Cloudland Canyon State Park, located in a mountain gorge with a cave for experienced spelunkers. Cottages with two nights minimum: 404-657-4050.

Features

The battlefield is the site of a 3-day battle where some of the most bitter Civil War fighting occurred. Chattanooga was then the key rail center and gateway to the Confederacy. Fighting began in June 1863, pitting General William S. Rosencrans' Army of the Cumberland against General Braxton Bragg's Confederates.

The ensuing battle resulted in over 18,000 Confederate dead or wounded. The Union had 16,000 casualties. By its end, Gen. Ulysses S. Grant was successful in forcing the Confederates to withdraw into Georgia, opening the route to Atlanta and the Confederacy.

The battlefield was established in 1890, and offers visitors the opportunity to study the operations of the two armies as they fought over all types of terrain. Observation towers have been placed on Missionary Ridge, Lookout Mountain, and on the Chickamauga Battlefield.

Activities

Obtain a map for the 7-mile car tour of the area at the visitors center, since the park contains separate areas: Chickamauga Battlefield, Point Park, Lookout Mountain Battlefield, Orchard Knob and Missionary Ridge. While at the center, see the large Fuller collection of American military arms.

The park has 40 miles of hiking trails including the Perimeter Trail, a 20-mile hike that covers much of the battlefield; Memorial Trail, 12 miles long, passing the point where eight brigade commanders died; and Confederate Line Trail, a 6-mile hike that passes through dense forest where the opposing forces met.

Information

Superintendent
Chickamauga and Chattanooga National Military Park
P.O. Box 2128
Ft. Oglethorp, GA 30742
404-866-9241

FT. FREDERICA NATIONAL MONUMENT

The monument is on St. Simons Island, and is connected to Brunswick by a toll causeway.

Airport

Brunswick-Malcolm McKinnon
Jacksonville Sectional
Latitude: 31–09
Longitude: 81–23
FSS: 912-638-8641
Car rentals

Accommodations

Holiday Inn, restaurant: 912-265-8830
Howard Johnson's Motor Lodge, restaurant open
    24 hours: 912-264-4720
Best Western Golden Isles, restaurant:
    912-264-0144
Ramada Inn, restaurant: 912-264-8611

Features

The English, under General James Oglethorpe's leadership, established a fort and settlement that lasted for 13 years. The fort was used to defend the colonists against England when it fought against Spain in 1742 in the War of Jenkins' Ear. The Battle of Bloody Marsh ended the fighting, and today you can see the Bloody Marsh Battle Site 6 miles south of the monument.

The settlement was destroyed by fire in 1758, and the last of the fort's soldiers left in 1763.

Activities

A visitors center is east of the townsite.

Tour Christ Church, south of the monument. It was established in the early 1800s.

The Museum of Coastal History is located in a former lighthouse keeper's house. The museum has exhibits telling of the island's early history. The view of the surrounding area from the lighthouse is also worth seeing.

Nearby Attraction

Visit Sea Island, which is accessible from St. Simons via a causeway. There you can enjoy golf, fishing, and tennis in a very picturesque setting.

Information

Superintendent
Fort Frederica National Monument
Route 4, Box 286-C
St. Simons Island, GA 31522
912-638-3639

KENNESAW MOUNTAIN NATIONAL BATTLEFIELD PARK

The park is 3 miles north of Marietta, Georgia, and 25 miles north of Atlanta.

Airport

McCollum, Atlanta Sectional
Latitude: 34–00

Longitude: 84–36
FSS: 404-691-2240
Car rental: Hertz: 404-422-4300
For other rentals: 404-422-4382, 2 miles from the park.

Macon-Herbert Smart Downtown, Atlanta Sectional
Latitude: 32–41
Longitude: 83–39
FSS: 912-788-5064, or 800-342-7284
Rental cars available.

Climate

The town has mild temperatures by Georgian standards because of its 1,100-foot elevation. It also experiences mild winters.

Accommodations

In Marietta:
    Holiday Inn: 404-952-8161
    La Quinta Motor Inn Northwest, restaurant: 404-951-0026
    Best Western-Bon Air Motel: 404-427-4676

In Kennesaw:
    Kennesaw Inn: 404-427-3181
    John Manns Motor Inn: 404-974-3586

Bed and Breakfast: Victorian Inns of Marietta/Atlanta: Marlow House, circa 1887 or Stanley House, circa 1895. Attend music recitals, Victorian readings or singalongs on weekday evenings and Sunday afternoons. Call 404-426-1887.

Camping is available in Acworth, Kennesaw, and Cartersville.

Features

The park was established to commemorate the 1864 Atlanta Campaign held during August when the city was placed under siege for a month. Atlanta was then the railroad hub and war manufacturing and storage center for the Confederates. Atlanta finally fell after much bitter fighting between General Sherman and General Joseph Johnston of the Confederates. Because of the victory of the Union forces here and in other areas, the Civil War's end came closer.

Activities

Take a self-guided car tour of the park, passing the major points of the battle. The tour begins at the visitors center and goes 4 miles to Cheatham Hill and then on to Kolb Farm. Stop along the way by various exhibits.

Hike the interpretative trails. One goes to the top of Kennesaw Mountain and is steep but rewarding with its panoramic view of the terrain so bitterly fought over.

Hike the trail on Pigeon Hill to see Confederate entrenchments and site of one of Sherman's major unsuccessful assaults.

The trail up Cheatham Hill passes the site of some of the fiercest fighting. You'll see the Confederate earthworks and markers indicating where prominent Union men fell.

The Kolb Farm house, built in 1836, was occupied by Union General Joseph Hooker after the battle. It's been restored to its former appearance, but is not open to the public.

Visit the Cyclorama of the Battle of Atlanta to see and hear the fighting reenacted.

While there, also see the *Texas*, the railroad engine that was featured in the famous locomotive chase on April 12, 1862. The other engine involved in this same raid, *The General* is in Kennesaw in the Big Charity Museum, and within 100 yards of where it was stolen.

Hiking trails include the park loop trail, 15$\frac{3}{5}$ miles long, which goes from the visitors center to Kolb Farm and returns. If you want to take shorter hikes along this trail, hike from the center to Mountaintop and back, a hike of 2 miles, or 5$\frac{2}{5}$ miles from the center to Burnt Hickory Road.

Take a walking/driving tour of historic Marietta. The town has 46 historic buildings, including the Kennesaw House-Hotel, circa 1855, and site of the meeting place for the Andrews Raiders the night before they stole the locomotive. Obtain a map from the Marietta Welcome Center, #2 Depot Street, Marietta, 404-429-1115

Information

Superintendent
Kennesaw Mountain National Battlefield Park
P.O. Box 1167
Marietta, GA 30061
404-427-4866

Nearby Attraction:

CHATTAHOOCHEE RIVER NATIONAL RECREATION AREA

The Chattahoochee River National Recreation Area is a 48-mile stretch of the river which passes Atlanta.

Accommodations

In Atlanta:
Marriott Interstate North Hotel: 404-952-7900
Ramada Inn: 404-952-7581
Holiday Inn-Powers Ferry Rd., restaurant: 404-955-1700

Bed and Breakfast:
Victorian Inns:
404-426-1886

Activities

You can go rafting and canoeing. Rentals are available from May to September from concessionaires at Johnsons Ferry and Powers Island. Others are available outside the park. Shuttle service is provided by the concessionaires from Johnsons Ferry, Powers Island, and Paces Mill. For information, call 404-394-6622.

The river's rapids are gentle and good for beginning rafters. Fishing is also good here, but swimming is not recommended.

The area has many good hiking trails, including Palisades Unit's Overlook Trail, Sope Creek, Gold Branch, Vickery Creek, and Island Ford Unit trails.

Information

Superintendent
1900 Northridge Rd.
Dunwoody, GA 30338
404-952-4419 or 404-394-7912

OCMULGEE NATIONAL MONUMENT

The monument is east of Macon, Georgia

Airports

Macon-Herbert Smart Downtown, Atlanta Sectional
Latitude: 32–41
Longitude: 83–39
FSS: 912-788-5064, or 800-342-7284
Car rentals

Lewis B. Wilson, Atlanta Sectional
Latitude: 32–41
Longitude: 83–39
FSS: 800-342-7284 or 912-788-5064

Accommodations

In Macon:
Best Western Town and Country: 912-781-7131
Ramada Inn, restaurant: 912-474-0871
Holiday Inn: restaurant: 912-788-0120
Red Carpet Inn: 912-781-2810

Features

A diorama in the museum shows a council of these farming Indians who lived here over 10 centuries ago. The mound builders lived in earth lodges.

The tribe built a ceremonial earthlodge in the center of town. As the leaders of the tribe began their ceremony, they drank *cassina*, an emetic made from the leaves of the yaupon shrub. They believed this purifies the body, cleansing it to be more receptive to the advice from the supernatural powers.

Activities

You can see seven temple mounds, once the religious hubs of the Indians who lived here. Indian crafts are demonstrated during the summer.

Hike 1 mile Opelota Nature Trail for an ecology tour of the swamp and forest, or drive along Temple Mound Drive to see the three largest mounds and the British trading post. At the Earthlodge, one of America's earliest public buildings, you can see the original 1,000-year-old clay floor with its seating for 47 villagers.

Information

Superintendent
Ocmulgee National Monument
1207 Emery Highway
Macon, GA 31201
912-742-0447

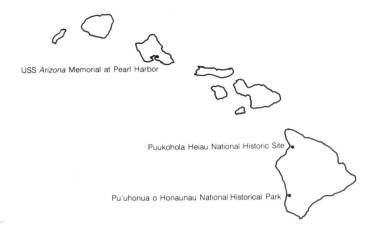

USS *Arizona* Memorial at Pearl Harbor

Puukohola Heiau National Historic Site

Pu'uhonua o Honaunau National Historical Park

Hawaii

PU'UHONUA O HONAUNAU NATIONAL HISTORICAL PARK

The park is 30 miles south of Ke-Ahole Airport, on the Big Island of Hawaii.

Airport

Kailua-Kona (Ke-Ahole Point)
Hawaiian-Mariana Sectional
Latitude: 19–44
Longitude: 156–02
FSS: 800-382-2281
Car rentals in Ke-Ahole:
    Alamo Rent-a-car: 800-327-9633
    American International Rent-a-car:
        808-329-2926
    Avis: 808-329-1745
    Budget: 808-329-8511

Access

By bus from Kailu, Kona.

Climate

It's sunny 95 percent of the time. The rainy season occurs during the summer. The area receives 25 inches of annual precipitation. The climate along the Kohala and Kona coasts is known for dry, calm, and sunny conditions year-round. Hilo receives more rain, generally at night.

Accommodations

In Captain Cook:
    Manago Hotel: 808-323-2642

In Kona:
    Mauna Kea Beach: 800-228-3000
    Kona Hilton Beach and Tennis Resort:
        808-329-3111
    Kona By The Sea: 808-329-0200
    Kona Lagoon: 808-322-2727
    Keauhoa Beach Hotel: 808-322-3441

Camping is available in the state park of Manuka, 20 miles south of the park.

Features

Pu'uhonua o Honaunau means ''Place of Refuge of Honanaunau.'' Hawaiian warriors or taboo-breakers once sought refuge from death by coming to this sacred place until 1819. Anyone breaking a *kapu*, a sacred rule of life, was immediately subject to punishment by death. These kapus included such rules as a common person not being allowed to walk in the chief's footsteps, touch any of his possessions, or even to let his shadow fall on the chief's palace grounds.

If a kapu breaker reached a pu'uhonna, a ceremony of absolution could be performed by the *kahuna pule*, or priest, and the offender was then permitted to return safely home.

Here you can see a twelfth-century sanctuary, wood carved figures, tikis, and St. Benedict's Church, often called the Painted Church because of its frescoed inner walls.

The grounds also include the great wall, which separated the palace grounds from the pu'uhonna.

Activities

See the prehistoric house sites (Fig. 9), the royal temple, and Great Wall that separated the palace grounds and royalty from the commoners. You can also see the royal fishpools, kept so that the chief always had fresh fish available.

Visitors can hike, swim, snorkel, fish, and follow a self-guided hiking trail through the park.

Attend the annual Establishment Day Cultural Festival the end of June. Enjoy playing Hawaiian games and tasting their special foods. For information, call 808-328-2288 or 808-328-2326.

Honaunau Bay near Pu'uhonua is one of the best snorkeling and scuba diving areas on the island. During the winter, however, high surf and severe storms can create hazardous ocean conditions.

Runners can run the Kilauea Volcano Marathon in January and the Rim Run at Volcanoes National Park in April.

The Merrie Monarch Festival features a statewide hula competition in Hilo.

Triathletes converge on the island in October to compete in the Iron Man Championship at Kailua-Kona.

Watch for humpback whales migrating through the area from November to March.

Hike ⅖ mile in Akaka Falls State Park to see the 442-foot falls.

In Kealakekua Bay State Underwater Park, you

Fig. 9. Skeletal frame for structure at Pu'uhonua o Honaunau National Historical Park.

can snorkel, scuba, or take a glass-bottom boat ride from Kailua-Kona.

Lapakahi State Historic Park has a reenactment of early Hawaiian life in the remains of an ancient coastal settlement.

Wailuku River State Park has the Boiling Pots, a succession of large pools connected underground, and 80-foot Rainbow Falls, best seen in the morning.

Information

Superintendent
Pu'uhonua O Honaunau National Historical Park
Honaunau, Kona, HI 96726
808-328-2326

PUUKOHOLA HEIAU NATIONAL HISTORIC SITE

The site is located on the northwest shore on the Big Island of Hawaii.

Airport

Kamuela-Waimea, Kohala,
Hawaiian-Mariana Sectional
Latitude: 20–00
Longitude: 156–58
FSS: 800-382-2281

It's 12 miles to the site.

Climate

Temperatures can reach the 90s. The area receives around 9 inches of annual precipitation.

Accommodations

Mauna Kea Beach Hotel: 808-882-7222
Camping at Spencer Beach Park.

Features

See the ruins of Puukohola Heiau, ''Temple on the Hill of the Whale.'' The temple platform was built of lava rocks and boulders without the use of mortar. It was built by King Kamehameha (1753–1819) during his rise to power.

Nearby is the Samuel M. Spencer Beach Park, which offers good snorkeling.

Activities

See two of the three temple ruins; the third one is submerged.

In August, attend the cultural festival celebrating the establishment of the temple.

USS *ARIZONA* MEMORIAL AT PEARL HARBOR

The memorial is off the Island of Oahu, west of the Honolulu Airport.

Airport

Honolulu International, Hawaiian-Mariana Sectional
Latitude: 21–19
Longitude: 157–55
FSS: 808-734-6677
Rental cars:
    Hertz: 808-836-2511, or 800-654-8200
    Avis: 808-836-5531
    Budget: 808-836-1700
    Thrifty: 808-836-2388

Access

You can either reach the memorial by private car or catch the Honolulu #20 bus from Waikiki. Get on the U.S.S. *Arizona* Memorial Shuttle or the Airport Motor Coach. Information: 808-926-4747.

Season

Open year-round, the monument is open Tuesday through Sunday from 8:00 A.M. to 3:00 P.M. It's closed Monday.

Accommodations

In Oahu:
    Great American Hotels in Hawaii: 808-922-3311

Hyatt Regency: 808-922-9292
Ilikai Hotel-Waikiki Beach: 808-949-3811
Hotel Corporation of the Pacific Islands: 808-922-3368
Aloha Surf: 808-923-0222

Features

The U.S.S. *Arizona* is the final resting place for over 1,177 men who died on December 7, 1941. The memorial was built over the sunken battleship.

Activities

Attend the 21-minute interpretive program at the visitors center while waiting your turn to board the Navy shuttle boat that takes you out to the memorial. You can remain on the memorial for as long as you wish, and catch the next available shuttle boat to return to the visitors center.

Look around the grounds of the center to see Ford Island, the focal point of the 1941 attack.

Additional Attractions in Oahu

Diamond Head State Monument in Honolulu contains a large tuff cone formed by a short series of volcanic explosions 100,000 years ago. Follow a 7/10-mile trail.

Snorkel or scuba in Nanauma Bay State Underwater Park, or in Hanauma Bay.

Iolani Palace State Monument in Honolulu is the royal palace of the Hawaiian monarchy. Guided tours Wednesday through Saturday by reservation: 808-536-2474.

Sacred Falls State Park offers a 2-mile hike to see the 80-foot falls. The trail is closed during rainy weather because of its location in a narrow canyon.

The blowhole near Koko Head is a good place to see large ocean waves force the water through a tiny hole in a lava ledge, blowing huge water geysers into the air.

Attend the Kodak Hula Show, presented outdoors at Kapiolani Park next to Waikiki Shell. Programs are given Tuesday, Wednesday, and Thursday from 10:00 A.M. on through the day. Shows are also presented on Fridays during the summer.

Visit Waimea Falls Park, located on the north shore of the island. See its botanical gardens with 46 bird species. It's open 10:00 A.M. until 5:30 P.M. For information, call 808-638-8511 or 808-923-8448.

Visit the Polynesian Cultural Center in Laie. The center features six native villages representing Hawaii, Fiji, New Zealand, Samoa, Tahiti, and Tonga.

Information

For general information from the Hawaiian Visitors Bureau regarding hotels, transportation, restaurants, and special events, call 808-923-1811.

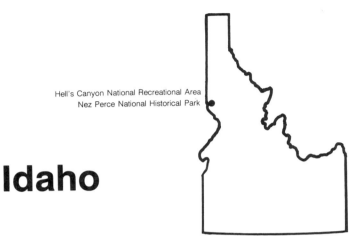

Hell's Canyon National Recreational Area
Nez Perce National Historical Park

Idaho

NEZ PERCE NATIONAL HISTORICAL PARK

The entire park covers approximately 400 miles, and the national park manages 4 sites out of 24. The 24 sites are located in Clearwater, Idaho, Lewis, and Nez Perce County in north central Idaho.

Airport

Lewiston Municipal, Great Falls Sectional
Latitude: 47–03
Longitude: 109–28
WS: 208-743-3841
Rental cars:
  Budget: 208-746-0488
  Hertz: 208-746-0411
  Rent-A-Dent: 208-746-3050

Climate

Annual rainfall is 13 inches. The area has hot summers and fairly mild winters. June through August temperatures average 82 degrees, but can reach as high as 110° F. January is the coldest month, with an average temperature of 31° F.

Accommodations

In Clarkston, WA:
  Sky Way Motel: 509-758-7351
  Astor Motel: 509-758-2509
  Sunset Motel: 509-758-2519
  Hacienda Lodge: 509-758-5583

In Lewiston, ID:
  Pony Soldier Motor Inn: 208-743-9526
  Best Western Tapadera Motor Inn:
    208-746-3311
  Sacajawea Lodge: 208-746-1393
  Sundance Motor Inn: 800-635-2225
    or 208-743-4501

Camping is available in three state parks within 25 miles of Spalding: Hellsgate, Winchester, and Chief Timothy, 8 miles from Clarkston. There are also National Forest campgrounds close by.

Features

The Nez Perce Indians, "pierced nose," were misnamed since they didn't pierce their noses at all.

They called themselves *Ne-Mee-Poo,* meaning "the people."

Their original territory covered northcentral Idaho, northeast Oregon, and southeast Washington. In 1855, they signed a treaty that maintained most of their original lands. But by 1860, gold had been discovered on some of their holdings, and prospectors began pouring onto the reservation. A new treaty was signed in 1863, reducing their reservation by 7 million acres.

Then, again in 1877, their lands were reduced by the "Severalty Act" passed by Congress, leaving the Indians with less than 12 percent of their 1863 Treaty Lands. Each Indian then was given title to 40 to 160 acres. The Indians now have become self-governed, with their own approved constitution and bylaws.

Activities

If you land in Lewiston, you can take a tour of one small segment of the park. Here you can see several historical sites including Donald Mackenzie's old trading post, Lenore Archaeological Site, which had been inhabited by the Indians for approximately 10,000 years, and St. Joseph's Mission, established in 1874.

Park headquarters are in Spalding, 11 miles east of Lewiston. There you can tour the Museum of Nez Perce Culture.

Visit the interpretative shelters at East Kamiah and White Bird Battlefield to see a panoramic view of the battleground where the Indians once defeated the U.S. Army.

Bicyclists will enjoy the bike paths along the Snake River levees in the Lewiston-Clarkston area. Hikers can explore some of the nearby National Forest trails.

Nearby Attractions

Hell's Canyon National Recreation Area: Take a boat trip up the Grand Canyon of the Snake River into the main part of Hell's Canyon, known as the deepest river gorge in North America. For information, call 208-743-3531.

For floating trips, contact Hell's Canyon Adventures: 503-785-3352; Snake River Outfitters: 208-799-8612, or Barker River Trips: 208-743-7459.

For jet boat trips into the canyon, contact S & S Outfitters at 208-746-3569, or the Snake River Outfitters: 208-799-8612.

Permits for boating the Snake River are required from the Friday before Memorial Day through September 15: 208-743-3648.

The recreation area also has approximately 1,000 miles of trails. Roads into the area may be rough and not open until mid-summer because of the snow. Check on current road conditions.

Take a summer tour from 2:00 to 5:00 P.M. on *Steamboat Jean,* an old paddlewheeler, one of the last to operate on the Columbia and Snake Rivers. It's moored in Hell's Gate State Park, 4 miles from town. Here you can also camp, fish, horseback ride, swim, water ski, hike, and bike along the 22-mile levee.

Information

Superintendent
Nez Perce National Historical Park
Spalding, ID 83551
208-843-2261

Superintendent
Hells Canyon National Recreation Area
208-743-3648

Illinois

Lincoln Home
National Historic Site

LINCOLN HOME NATIONAL HISTORIC SITE

The site is in downtown Springfield at 526 Seventh Street. Visitors center: 426 Seventh.

Airport

Springfield-Capital, St. Louis Sectional
Latitude: 39–50
Longitude: 89–40
WS: 217-525-4252
FSS: 217-528-4335
Car rentals:
    Avis: 800-333-1800 or 217-522-7728
    Hertz: 800-654-3131 or 217-525-8820
    National: 800-328-4567 or 217-544-6300

Accommodations

Howard Johnson's Motor Lodge, restaurant: 217-529-9100
Best Western State House Inn, restaurant: 217-523-5661
Springfield Super 8 Motel: 217-528-8889 or 800-255-3050
Motel 6: 789-0520

Camping: There are eight lake parks around Lake Springfield and camping is available here. Camping is also available in Riverside Park beside Sangamon River, at Lake Victoria Campground, Springfield KOA, and Sangchris Lake State Park.

Features

The home is the only one that Lincoln ever owned, and was built in 1839. He lived here for 17 years. Many of the furnishings are originals.

Activities

Tour Lincoln's home and visitors center (Fig. 10).

Attend one of the Great American People Shows, "Your Obedient Servant A. Lincoln," "Abraham Lincoln Walks at Midnight," or "Even We Here," at the New Salem State Park from mid-June to mid-August. It's presented nightly at 8:00 P.M. except Monday. Information: 217-632-7755.

Visit the Lincoln Tomb State Historic Site at Oak Ridge Cemetery. It's the burial site for Lincoln and his family and has an extensive collection of Lincoln and Civil War sculptures.

The area has other historical homes open for touring including the Dana-Thomas house designed by Frank Lloyd Wright, Edwards Place, Governor's Mansion, and the Vachel Lindsay home.

Go to the Lincoln Depot, where he bade farewell to the town when he left to be inaugurated as president.

The Lincoln family pew is located in the First Presbyterian Church. It's open weekdays.

See Lincoln's original law office in the Herndon Building.

Fig. 10. Lincoln Home National Historic Site. (National Park Service Photo)

The original ledger containing Lincoln's account is on display at the Lincoln Ledger Marine Bank.

The Lincoln Memorial Garden and Nature Center offers a 5-mile hiking trail.

See the Thomas Rees Memorial Carillon, one of the largest of its kind in the world. Tours are offered daily in the summer from 2:00 to 8:00 P.M., and from 2:00 to 8:00 P.M. weekends in May, September, and October. Concerts are performed May to October on Saturday, Sunday and Wednesday at 7:00 P.M. and from November through April on Saturday and Sunday at 4:00 P.M.

At the Lincoln New Salem Park, 20 miles northwest of Springfield, you can see a reconstructed log cabin village where Lincoln spent his early adult years. Attend the Great American People Show there from mid-June through mid-August. Information: 217-632-7755.

Lake Springfield offers opportunities for boating, canoeing, and fishing.

Information

Superintendent
Lincoln Home National Historic Site
426 7th St.
Springfield, IL 62701
217-789-2357

Nearby Attraction

Attend Christmas celebrations at the Lincoln's New Salem State Historic Site in Petersburg. This is the log village where young Abraham Lincoln tended the store while also serving as its postmaster. For information, call 217-632-7953.

Indiana

Lincoln Boyhood
National Monument

LINCOLN BOYHOOD NATIONAL MONUMENT

The monument is 4 miles south of Dale.

Airport

Perry County Municipal, St. Louis Sectional
Latitude: 38–01
Longitude: 86–41
FSS: 812-683-3646
Taxi

Huntingburg, St. Louis Sectional
Latitude: 38–14
Longitude: 86–57
FSS: 812-877-2571
Taxi

Accommodations

In Huntingburg:
    Wayside Motel: 812-683-3636
    Dutchman Inn-Best Western: 812-683-2334

In Dale:
    Stone's Motel: 812-937-4448
    Lincoln Motel: 812-937-4361

    Camping: Lincoln State Park, Lincoln City, Forest Service Tell City

Features

Thomas Lincoln had lost his land in a title dispute three times prior to moving to Indiana in 1816. Here he gradually paid for the land on which he and his family lived.

His first wife Nancy died in 1818. In 1819, he married Sarah Bush Johnson. The family stayed in Indiana until 1829, when they decided to move on to Illinois.

Activities

Hike the Historic Trail of Stones, which points out the major events in the Lincoln family's lives.

Visit the gravesite of Nancy Hanks Lincoln, Abraham's mother. Also see the Lincoln Living Historical Farm, a working pioneer farmstead with costumed "pioneers" re-enacting life in the 1800s. Tours are offered from mid-April through October (Fig. 11).

Enjoy camping, hiking, boating, and fishing in Lincoln State Park, which joins the monument.

Information

Superintendent
Lincoln Boyhood National Monument
Lincoln City, IN 47552
812-937-4757

Fig. 11. Lincoln Boyhood National Monument. (National Park Service Photo)

Iowa

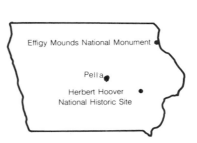

EFFIGY MOUNDS NATIONAL MONUMENT

The monument is located on the high bluffs across the Mississippi River near Prairie du Chien, Wisconsin.

Airport

Prairie du Chien Municipal
Chicago Sectional
Latitude: 43–01
Longitude: 91–07
FSS: 608-784-3170
Car rentals

Season

Open year-round. Tours are offered during the summer only.

Accommodations

In Prairie du Chien:
Brisbois Motor Inn: 608-326-8404
Holiday Motel: 608-326-2448
Prairie Motel: 608-326-6461

Features

The area is located along the Upper Mississippi River Valley. It has 183 known burial mounds, created 2,000 years ago by the prehistoric Indians who lived in the area from 500 B.C. to 1400 A.D. Most of the mounds are conical or linear, but 27 of them are different and resemble the shapes of birds and animals (Fig. 12). One of the mounds, the Great Bear, is 137 feet long and 70 feet across.

It's believed the Indians carefully formed the earth effigies to be most fitting for the departed. Around 12,000 years ago, these Paleo-Indians in Iowa killed huge elephantine mammals and extinct forms of bison.

Three mounds left by the Hopewell Indians, who lived in the area from 100 B.C. to 600 A.D., are adjacent to the visitors center.

Activities

Take the self-guided trail that goes through the burial mounds. Guided tours are available during the summer.

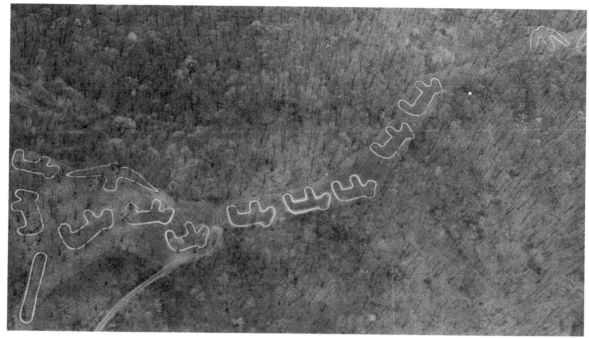

Fig. 12. "Marching Bear" mound, Effigy Mounds National Monument. (National Park Service Photo)

Information

Superintendent
Effigy Mounds National Monument
P.O. Box K
McGregor, IA 52157
319-873-2356

TULIP TIME IN PELLA

If you're in Iowa the second weekend in May, stop in Pella for their famed celebration of Tulip Time. The small Dutch community features Dutch dancing and parades offered Thursday through Saturday. The parade is also shown at night when it's lit. Be sure to pick up some delicious Dutch pastries at the local bakery.

Airport

Pella Municipal, Chicago Sectional
Latitude: 41–27
Longitude: 92–56

FSS: 800-532-1487
Car rentals

Accommodations

In Pella:
  Pella Motor Inn: 319-628-9500
  Dutch Mill Motel: 319-628-1060

In Knoxville:
  Lakeland Motel: 319-842-7155, reservations necessary.

HERBERT HOOVER NATIONAL HISTORIC SITE

The site is in West Branch.

Airport

Iowa City Municipal, Chicago Sectional
Latitude: 41–38

Longitude: 91–33
FSS: 800-332-5241
Car rentals: 356-5045 or call Iowa City Flying Service: 319-338-7543

Accommodations

In Iowa City:
    Alamo Friendship Inn, restaurant: 319-354-4000
    Best Western Abbey Inn, restaurant, airport transportation: 319-351-6324
    The Ironmen Inn, restaurant: 319-351-6600

    Camping: Cedar River, Edgewater, and Lake Macbride.

Features

The site has several historic structures including the restored two-room cottage where Hoover was born, a replica of his father's blacksmith shop, and West Branch's first school, restored to circa 1870. It also has the Herbert Hoover Presidential Library and Museum.

Activities

Tour the Herbert Hoover Library and Museum and see memorabilia relating to his 50 years of public service. Movies on Hoover's life are presented June to August.

Hike the H. H. Prairie Trail, a 1³⁄₁₀-mile-long trail through the original grassland that covered the area prior to its cultivation in the mid-1800s. You pass two old farms, circa 1879 and 1909.

Information

Superintendent
Herbert Hoover National Historic Site
P.O. Box 607
West Branch, IA 52358-0607
319-643-5301

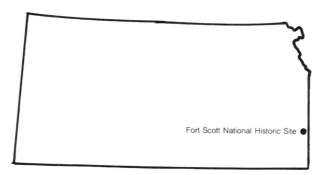

Kansas

FORT SCOTT NATIONAL HISTORIC SITE

The fort is 5 miles from the Missouri border in eastern Kansas.

Airport

Fort Scott Municipal, Kansas City Sectional
Latitude: 37–47
Longitude: 94–46
FSS: 800-362-0399

Accommodations

In Fort Scott:
    Best Western Fort Scott Inn: 316-223-0100
    Colonial Motel: 316-223-0200
    Red Ram Motel: 316-223-2400

Camping: KOA

Features

The fort is a restored frontier military fort that was in operation from 1842-1853, and includes a post hospital, guardhouse, barracks, and some other buildings (Fig. 13). Its original purpose was to keep the peace between nomadic tribes, relocated Indians from the east, and white settlers. The soldiers also guarded caravans traveling along the Santa Fe Trail. By 1853, these activities were no longer necessary, and the garrison was transferred to Leavenworth.

Activities

On special weekends from May to October, you can watch life recreated as it was in the frontier outpost. The first weekend in June features the Good Ol' Days with an 1899 Street Fair. The Bourbon County Fair is in July, and October's Pioneer Harvest Fiesta features early gas and steam engines. The first weekend of December features Victorian home tours.

Drive past the homes constructed in the 1890s, and visit Fort Lincoln School. Visit the cemetery and locate the graves of Indian scouts Stick Out Belly and Deer in Water.

Information

Superintendent
Fort Scott National Historic Site
Old Fort Blvd.
Fort Kansas, KS 66701
316-223-0310

Fig. 13. Ft. Scott National Historic Site. (National Park Service Photo)

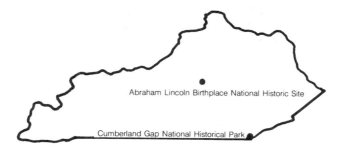

Abraham Lincoln Birthplace National Historic Site

Cumberland Gap National Historical Park

Kentucky

ABRAHAM LINCOLN BIRTHPLACE NATIONAL HISTORIC SITE

The site is 3 miles south of Hodgenville.

Airport

Elizabethtown, St. Louis Sectional
Latitude: 37–41
Longitude: 85–55
FSS: 800-752-6087
Car rentals:
　　Budget: 502-737-2161

Accommodations

In Elizabethtown:
　　Motel 6: 502-769-3376
　　Holiday Best Western Motel: 502-765-2111
　　Holiday Inn North: 502-769-2344

Camping: Cruise Inn or Salem Lake.

Features

In 1809, Lincoln was born in the small log cabin erected on land referred to as Sinking Spring Farm.

Lincoln's father paid $200 cash for the 300 acres of land. The family lived here until 1811 before moving to Knob Creek, 10 miles northeast. A granite memorial shrine encloses the log cabin.

Activities

You can visit the three Lincoln homes around Elizabethtown: Lincoln Heritage House, Birthplace, and Lincoln Boyhood Home on Knob Creek Farm. Each Saturday at 8:30, attend the Lincoln Jamboree presented adjacent to the Lincoln Birthplace.

Attend Founders Day Weekend, held the weekend nearest to July 17, and watch special demonstrations and two musical programs.

In mid-October, attend the annual Lincoln Days Celebration with a parade, rail splitting, and pioneer games.

Nearby Attractions

West of town is Rough River Lake and Nolin Lake where you can boat, fish, and water ski.

Tour nearby Ft. Knox military reservation, General George C. Patton Museum of Cavalry and Armor, and the U.S. Gold Depository, with gold valued over $20 billion.

Churchill Downs is an historic thoroughbred racing track and home of the Kentucky Derby.

Tour My Old Kentucky Home, a Georgian colonial mansion built in the 1800s.

See The Stephen Foster Story, an outdoor museum drama offered from mid-June through Labor Day.

Tour Mammoth Cave.

The Coca Cola Memorabilia Museum contains the largest collection of Coca Cola antiques dating back to 1886.

Information

Superintendent
Abraham Lincoln Birthplace National Historic Site
RFD 1
Hodgenville, KY 42748
502-358-3874

Chamber of Commerce: 502-765-4334

CUMBERLAND GAP NATIONAL HISTORICAL PARK

The park is southeast of Middlesboro, Kentucky, in the mountains where Kentucky, Tennessee, and Virginia meet.

Airport

Middlesboro Bell County, Cincinnati Sectional
Latitude: 36–36
Longitude: 83–44
FSS: 800-442-7883
Car rentals

Accommodations

In Middlesboro:
    Best Western Inn: 606-248-5630
    Quality Motel: 606-869-3681
    Holiday Inn: 606-869-3631

In Cumberland Gap:
    Holiday Inn: 615-869-3631

Camping: Pine Mountain State Park

Climate

The summer weather is hot and humid. Winters can be very cold.

Features

Dr. Thomas Walker found this natural gap through the Cumberland Mountains, and in 1769 Daniel Boone blazed the Wilderness Trail through here (Fig. 14). By the 1800s, many of the pioneers crossed the Appalachians using this gap. The gap was also important during the Civil War, and some of the early fortifications are still there.

Activities

The visitors center is near the Middlesboro entrance. It offers memorabilia from the Civil War and early pioneer days.

The park has about 50 miles of hiking trails. Many of the park features such as Sand Cave and White Rocks are only accessible by trail; 16-mile-long Ridge Trail, which gives the visitor some great looks over the valley, is accessible on foot only. It has three primitive campsites.

Drive to Pinnacle Overlook to see into three states.

You can also walk through Hensley Settlement, a restored pioneer community similar to those founded by the early settlers to the area. At one time, around 100 people lived here, but it was gradually abandoned. Today, 25 of the early buildings have been restored, and you can watch demonstrations of how the people now living there work their fields with horse-drawn equipment. It's accessible via a 4-mile hike up the Chadwell Gap Trail. Pick up a map at the park headquarters.

Enjoy a float trip on the Cumberland River in the Cumberland Falls State Resort Park between May and October, and see a 125-foot waterfall.

Information

Superintendent
Cumberland Gap National Historical Park
P.O. Box 840
Middlesboro, KY 40965
606-248-2817

Fig. 14. Cumberland Gap National Historical Park. (National Park Service Photo)

Nearby Attractions
In Corbin and London

Airport

London-Corbin, Cincinnati Sectional
Latitude: 37–05
Longitude: 84–04
FSS: 800-442-7883

Accommodations

In Corbin:
Holiday Inn 606-528-6301

Quality Inn: 606-528-4802
Knights Inn: 606-523-1500

Activities

Attend the Nibroc Festival in Corbin in August and enjoy a parade, display of arts and crafts, and square dancing.

In London, visit Levi Jackson Wilderness Road State Park, where a bloody Indian massacre occurred. Boone's Trace passes through here, and in the late 1700s, many pioneers followed his road.

Tour the Mountain Life Museum to see artifacts from the pioneering days. It's open from May through October.

Louisiana

Jean LaFitte National Historical Park

CHALMETTE NATIONAL HISTORICAL PARK AND JEAN LAFITTE NATIONAL HISTORICAL PARK

This park includes Barataria, an area of bayou, swamp and marsh, Chalmette National Historical Park, and the French Quarter.

Barataria is on the west bank of the Mississippi and is a wetlands area where the ancient cultures of Troyville, Marksville, and Tchefuncte were located. You can take self-guided tours beginning at Bayou Coquille. Be prepared for wet ground and insects.

Chalmette National Historical Park is in St. Bernard Parish and 6 miles from New Orleans. If you land at Lakefront, the park is approximately 15 miles away.

Airports

New Orleans-Lakefront, New Orleans Sectional
Latitude: 30–02
Longitude: 90–01
FSS: 504-528-9393 or 504-528-9842
Rental cars:
    Avis: 800-331-1800 or 504-245-1140
    Hertz: 800-654-3131 or 504-242-3214

Dollar: 504-468-3643
International: 504-524-4645

New Orleans International (Moisant Field), New Orleans Sectional
Latitude: 29–59
Longitude: 29–59
FSS: 504-528-9842
Rental cars:
    Avis: 800-331-1800 or 504-464-9511
    Hertz: 800-654-3131 or 504-468-3695
    Budget: 504-464-0311

Climate

The summers can be hot and humid. The winters are mild.

Accommodations

In New Orleans:
    Days Inn at New Orleans Airport, airport transportation, restaurant: 504-469-2531
    Best Western International, restaurant: 504-466-1401
    Holiday Inn at the Airport, restaurant: 504-467-5611

Howard Johnson's at the Airport, airport transportation: 504-885-5700

In the French Quarter:
Hotel Provincial: 504-581-4995 or 800-535-7922
Chateau Motor Hotel: 504-524-9636
Dauphine Orleans Motor Hotel: 504-586-1800

Camping: Fountainbleau State Park on north shore of Lake Pontchartrain, and in St. Bernard Park.

Features

Chalmette Park is the location of a great victory obtained during the Battle of New Orleans in the War of 1812, and includes a national cemetery (Fig. 15).

Activities

Tour Chalmette, and see the visitors center housed in the Beauregard Home built in the 1830s.

Access to the Chalmette Cemetery is within walking distance from Tour Stop 5, or by car from St. Bernard Highway ½ mile east of the entrance.

In mid-January, around the 11th and 12th, attend the Anniversary of the Battle of New Orleans held on the Chalmette Battlefield. Watch the recreation of life as it was originally experienced in the military encampment.

Drive the 1½-mile road that begins at the park entrance and has six stops which interpret the important features of the battlefield.

Take a cruise aboard the Bayou Jean Lafitte from Toulouse Street Wharf at Jackson. The cruise passes the park and continues through the Algiers Lock, returning through the Harvey Canal. The trip takes 5 hours and departs daily at 11:00 A.M. For information, call 504-586-8777.

A cruise aboard the Natchez, an authentic Sternwheeler Steamboat, takes 2 hours, passing Chalmette, but not making a stop. For information, call 425-SAIL.

Participate in the annual reenactment of the steamboat race from New Orleans to St. Louis. Trip

Fig. 15. Chalmette National Historical Park, site of a great battle during the Battle of New Orleans.

options can be for two to twelve nights, and the boat may be boarded at various stops along the route. For information, call the Delta Queen Steamboat Co. at 1-800-543-1949.

French Quarter: Take a walking tour and see many quaint shops, restaurants, and homes built in the 1800s. The Quarter is only 13 blocks long and five to ten blocks deep. It's also an interesting place to stay, since you can tour everything easily on foot, walk down to the Mississippi River to take a riverboat cruise, or catch a streetcar and ride 13⅓ miles to see many antebellum homes. The streetcar is 150 years old and takes 45 minutes to ride to the end of the line.

Be sure to go inside the Jackson Brewery, now redone to house 30 stores and 11 cafes. Nearby is Jackson Square, where band concerts are given on Sundays from 2:00 to 5:00 P.M. during the summer months.

You can also catch a bus from the Quarter to Longue Vue and tour the house and gardens circa 1939-42. The grounds contain beautiful gardens, one section designed to resemble Generalife Gardens of the Alhambra in Spain (Fig. 16).

Attend a Brown Bag concert offered year-round in Lafayette Square every Wednesday from 11:30 A.M. to 1:00 P.M. Information: 523-1465.

Open air concerts are given in the French Market Alley at St. Phillips Street every Saturday and Sunday from 1:00 to 3:00 P.M. They're also available in Jackson Square in front of St. Louis Cathedral Sundays from 2:00 to 5:00 P.M.

Enjoy boating and fishing in Lake Pontchartrain. For boat information: 504-282-8111 or 504-568-5664. The area also offers good hiking and biking.

Attend Mardi Gras and become part of the festively costumed crowds and pre-Lenten activities, culminating on Mardi Gras Day. Information: Greater New Orleans Tourist and Convention Com-

Fig. 16. Longue Vue House, New Orleans. A classical style house furnished with eighteenth- and nineteenth-century antiques and surrounded by beautiful gardens.

mission, Inc., 1520 Sugar Bowl Dr., New Orleans, 70112, 504-566-5011. For a parade schedule, call the Tourist Commission at 504-568-5661.

Tour the Superdome, home to the New Orleans Saints. Tours are every hour from 9 to 4. For information, call 504-587-3810.

Information

Unit Manager
Chalmette National Historical Park
St. Bernard Hwy.
Chalmette, LA 70043
504-271-8186

Jean Lafitte National Historical Park
400 Royal St.
Room 200
New Orleans, LA 70130
504-589-3882

Roosevelt Campobello International Park

Maine

ROOSEVELT CAMPOBELLO INTERNATIONAL PARK

The park is in northeastern Maine on Campobello Island across Lubec Narrows. Access is from Lubec over the Franklin D. Roosevelt Memorial Bridge.

Airport

Lubec Municipal, Halifax Sectional
Latitude: 44–50
Longitude: 67–02
FSS: 800-432-7365

Accommodations

Homeport Inn: 207-733-2077
Eastland Motel: 207-733-5501

Features

Campobello Park is a 3,000-acre memorial park with the 34-room home where Roosevelt spent most of his summers from 1905 to 1921.

Activities

The home is open from May to October.

Information

506-752-2997

Nearby Attractions

Visit Quoddy Head State Park, where you can hike along the trails. Also see the West Quoddy Lighthouse built in 1808.

At nearby Eastport, record tides have been recorded with a variation of up to 26 feet.

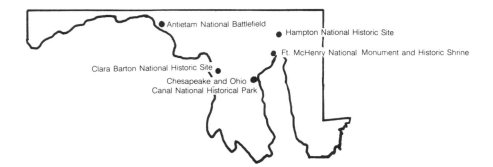

Maryland

ANTIETAM NATIONAL BATTLEFIELD

The battlefield is located 1 mile north of Sharpsburg, and 10 miles south of Hagerstown.

Airport

Hagerstown, Washington County Regional Washington Sectional
Latitude: 39–42
Longitude: 77–43
FSS: 304-263-9353
Rental cars:
    Hertz: 800-654-3131 or 301-739-6117
    Avis: 301-733-1277
    Kirk Ford: 301-678-6123

Transportation to the park from Hagerstown via the County Commuter bus from Peoples Drug Store on the square, Wednesday and Saturday at 9:30 A.M. and 3:45 P.M. Information: 301-791-3047.

Accommodations

In Hagerstown:
    Sheraton Inn: 301-790-3010
    Ramada Inn: 301-733-5100
    Quality Inn: 301-739-6100

Bed and Breakfast: Inn at Antietam: 432-6601

In Shepherdstown:
    Bavarian Inn: 304-873-2551

Campgrounds near the Antietam Battlefield: Antietam Creek, McCoy's Ferry, and Spring Gap.

Features

The Battle of Sharpsburg occurred here on September 17, 1862. This was the bloodiest day of the Civil War, in which over 12,000 Union soldiers and approximately 11,000 Confederates were wounded or killed. The Union was then led by McClellan, who defeated Lee's army at a time when Lee had hoped to invade northern land.

The battle also resulted in the President's issuance of the Emancipation Proclamation, freeing all the slaves living in states fighting against the United States. Thus the war now had two purposes: to maintain the Union and to end slavery.

Activities

The battlefield has interpretative markers and monuments along with Dunker Church, which dates back to 1852. Watch presentations of military life weekends from June through October.

Hike the self-guided historic nature trail.

Follow the self-guided 8-mile auto tour.

Hike the historic trail developed for the scouts. Maps are available at the visitors center.

Visit the Antietam National Cemetery in Sharpsburg, established in 1865, containing the graves of 4,763 Union soldiers and 281 additional graves of men who died in later wars.

Information

Superintendent
Antietam National Battlefield
P.O. Box 158
Sharpsburg, MD 21782-0158
301-432-5124

CHESAPEAKE AND OHIO CANAL NATIONAL HISTORICAL PARK

The park follows the Maryland side of the Potomac River beginning in Georgetown, Washington D.C., and goes to Cumberland, Maryland.

Airports

Portsmouth-Hampton Roads
Washington Sectional
Latitude: 36–46
Longitude: 76–26
FSS: 804-855-3029.
Car rentals

Waynesboro, Washington Sectional
Latitude: 38–05
Longitude: 78–57
FSS: 800-572-6000

Accommodations

In Frederick:
Best Western Red Horse Motor Inn, restaurant: 301-662-0281
Holiday Inn, restaurant: 301-662-5141
Sheraton Motor Inn, restaurant: 301-694-7500

In Hagerstown:
Holiday Inn, restaurant: 301-739-9050
Ramada Inn, restaurant: 301-733-5100

In Shepherdstown:
Bavarian Inn and Lodge: 304-876-2551
Shang-Ra-La Retreat: 304-876-2391
Inn at Antietam: 304-432-6601

In Harper's Ferry:
Cliffside Motor Inn: 301-535-6302
Hilltop House Hotel: 304-535-6321

Features

The canal was begun in 1824 and its 184½ miles of canals were most active in the 1870s, when as many as 540 boats floated through its channels. Along the route you can see 74 lift locks, 11 aqueducts, and many historic lockhouses. Be sure to see the Monocacy Aqueduct near Dickerson, and Paw Paw Tunnel near Paw Paw, West Virginia.

The canal was originally planned to connect the federal capitol on the Potomac with Pittsburgh on the Ohio River. Eventually steam railroads began replacing the barges, which were finally discontinued in 1974. The canal had reached Cumberland, where it was to cross the Alleghenies, but stockholders decided to quit and the project was discontinued.

Activities

Overfly the area and watch for the Great Falls of the Potomac located approximately 15 miles northwest of Washington D.C. This area is a favorite for hikers, bicyclists, and canoeists.

Take a barge drawn by mules from the visitors center at the Great Falls Tavern in Potomac. You can also begin this trip from the canal in Georgetown at the landing between Thomas Jefferson Street and 30th St. Information: 301-299-2026, or 202-472-4376.

Visit the Great Falls Tavern and Museum to view exhibits on the history of the canal. The area is accessible via exit 41 off I-495 (Capitol Beltway) at the end of MacArthur Blvd. Here you can also watch two films, *Down the Old Potomac* and *The C&O Canal*, which are shown continuously.

An elevated 185-mile towpath goes beside the Potomac River where camping, picnicking, bicycling, hiking, and running are popular activities. The path becomes slippery after heavy rain, and portions may be washed out. Hiker-Biker Campsites are available every 5 miles along the route from Carderock to Cumberland.

Three sections are particularly recommended for bike trips: Great Falls Tavern to Georgetown, 15 Mile Creek to Paw Paw Tunnel, or 24 miles from Dam 4 to Lock 33.

Canoeing on the Potomac is only recommended for experienced canoeists. Popular spots are between Georgetown and Violetts Lock near Seneca, Mile 0-22. Portage is required around the locks. It's also good at Big Pool, Mile 112, Little Pool, Mile 120, and at Torn Creek to Oldtown, Mile 126-127.

Visit C&O's Paw Paw Tunnel near the north end of the path. Take a 20-minute walk through the tunnel, built to eliminate six sets of bends in the Potomac River. There is a nature trail along the tunnel hill for exploration.

Go to Chesapeake City to visit the C&O Museum and watch a working model of a water wheel and lock. Closed Sundays and holidays.

Tour Harper's Ferry National Historic Park, site of John Brown's raid during the Civil War. Climb to Overlook Cliff on the Maryland Heights for a memorable view of the river. Take a 3½-hour walk along the trail passing the ruins of Civil War fortifications.

Information

Superintendent
C&O Canal National Historical Park
P.O. Box 4
Sharpsburg, MD 21782
301-739-4200

CLARA BARTON NATIONAL HISTORIC SITE

Clara Barton's home is in Glen Echo (Fig. 17).

Airports

Dulles International
Washington Sectional
Latitude: 38–56
Longitude: 77–27
FSS: 202-347-4040
WS: 703-661-8526
Car rentals

Washington National
Washington Sectional
Latitude: 38–51
Longitude: 77–02
FSS: 202-347-4040
Car rentals

Fig. 17. Glen Echo House, home of Clara Barton.

Features

Clara Barton was the founder and first president of the American Red Cross. Her home is still furnished with her possessions.

Activities

The site itself is open daily from 10:00 A.M. to 5:00 P.M. with the exception of New Year's Day, Thanksgiving, and Christmas. Her home, however, is not open every day, so call 301-492-6245 for information on hours and tours.

While in Glen Echo, visit Glen Echo Park, which was formerly an amusement park, but now arts and cultural events are featured. On Wednesdays and weekends from May to September, you can ride the hand-carved Dentzel Carousel. On Sundays, artists' workshops are taught year-round. For information, call 301-492-6282.

Information

Superintendent
George Washington Memorial Parkway
Turkey Run Park
McLean, VA 22101
301-492-6246

FORT McHENRY NATIONAL MONUMENT AND HISTORIC SHRINE

The monument is 3 miles from Baltimore on Whetstone Point. Easy access is over East Fort Avenue.

Airport

Martin State, Washington Sectional
Latitude: 39–19
Longitude: 76–25
FSS: 301-766-0757
WS: 301-859-7257
Rental cars:
 Avis: 301-685-6000
 Budget: 301-837-6955
 Hertz: 301-859-3600

Accommodations

In Baltimore:
 Holiday Inn, Inner Harbor: 301-685-3500
 Ramada Hotel: 301-265-1100
 Sheraton Johns Hopkins Inn: 301-675-6800

Bed and Breakfast: The Traveller: 301-269-6232

Features

Ft. McHenry guards the approaches to Baltimore from the Patapsco River and Chesapeake Bay, and was constructed between 1789 and 1803 to protect Baltimore's interior harbor.

During the War of 1812, the fort was bombarded for 25 hours by the British. Key watched from another ship, and after the shelling ended, was inspired by the sight of the Stars and Stripes still waving to write the words that later became part of our national anthem.

The fort resembles its pre-Civil War days and the American flag is flown 24 hours a day.

Activities

Shuttle boat service to the monument leaves from the Inner Harbor every half hour: 301-752-1515

Stop by the visitors center to watch their movie, *The Star Spangled Banner,* and then see the exhibits and military memorabilia. Take a self-guided tour of the star-shaped fort and grounds, or a guided one during the summer. See the flagpole where the 42-by-30-foot battle flag was flying during the bombardment.

Additional Attractions

See Mary Pickersgill's Star Spangled Banner Flag Home. She hand-sewed the flag that flew over Ft. McHenry during the War of 1812. Information: 301-837-1793.

Babe Ruth Birthplace Museum is on 216 Emory Street. See films on his life and of the Baltimore Orioles as they played in the World Series. Information: 301-727-1539.

Edgar Allan Poe's grave and house is in Baltimore. Tours of the cemetery are available the first and third Friday evening and Saturday mornings. The house is open from April through mid-December. Cemetery information: 301-528-7228. House information: 301-396-7932.

Climb up the Washington Monument, a 178-foot column with 229 steps, to get a good overlook of the city. Friday to Tuesday, 10:00 A.M. to 4:00 P.M.

In mid-January, see the Chesapeake Bay Boat Show, which features one of the largest boat displays on the East coast. Information: 301-383-1200.

Bike along the 8-mile bike path in Herring River Park.

Take a 3-hour excursion aboard the Clipper City sailing ship from June 15 to October 15: 301-539-6063. Take a luncheon or dinner cruise year-round aboard the *Lady Baltimore*. For information, call 301-727-3113.

Tour nearby Frederick with its 33 blocks that are part of a National Historic District. It was founded in 1745 by English and German settlers, and has many colonial mansions.

Information

Superintendent
Fort McHenry
National Monument and Historic Shrine
Baltimore, MD 21230
301-962-4290

HAMPTON NATIONAL HISTORIC SITE

The historic site is located outside Baltimore in Towson. Access from Baltimore is from the Beltway I-695. Follow the signs.

Airports

Glenn L. Martin State, Washington Sectional
Latitude: 39–19
Longitude: 76–25
FSS: 301-347-4040
WS: 301-859-7257

Car rentals:
Avis: 301-685-6000
Budget: 301-837-6955
Hertz: 301-859-3600

Essex Skypark, Washington Sectional
Latitude: 39–15
Longitude: 76–26
FSS: 301-760-7950
No car rentals

Accommodations

In Towson:
Econo Lodge Towson: 301-892-0900
Quality Inn: 301-825-9100
Welcome Inn: 301-668-7100
Towson East Motel: 301-825-5800

Features

The mansion was one of the largest ornate mansions built during the post-Revolutionary War period and dates back to 1783 (Fig. 18). The Ridgely family lived here for 158 years. The orangerie once contained one of the best citrus collections in the United States.

Activities

Tour the picturesque Georgian mansion built in the late 18th century and enjoy the beautiful grounds. The site is closed Mondays, and open Tuesday through Saturday from 11:30 A.M. to 4:30 P.M. and on Sunday from 1:00 to 5:00 P.M.

Refreshments are available in the tearoom 11:30 A.M. to 3:00 P.M.

Information

Superintendent
Hampton National Historic Site
535 Hampton Lane
Towson, MD 21204
301-823-7054

Fig. 18. Georgian mansion built in 1783 for the Ridgely family, Hampton National Historic Site.

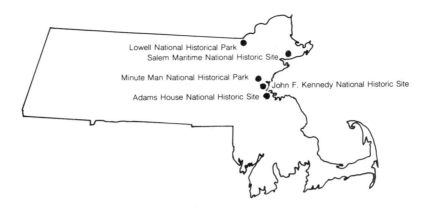

Lowell National Historical Park
Salem Maritime National Historic Site
Minute Man National Historical Park
John F. Kennedy National Historic Site
Adams House National Historic Site

Massachusetts

ADAMS HOUSE NATIONAL HISTORIC SITE

The site is on 135 Adams Street, Quincy, Massachusetts. The John Adams and John Quincy Adams Birthplaces are a short distance away at 141 Franklin Street. Quincy is 8 miles south of Boston.

Access from Boston: Take Exit 24, Furnace Brook Parkway, on the Southeast Expressway, MA 93. If you take rapid transit from Boston, take the Red Line to Quincy.

Season

The Adams National Historic Site is open daily 9:00 A.M. to 5:00 P.M., April 19 to November 10. The John Adams and John Quincy Adams Birthplaces are open April 19 to October 15.

Accommodations

President's City Motel: 617-479-6500

Features

The historic site includes the house, library, garden, and stables. It's been continuously occupied for four centuries by the Adams family, from 1788 to 1924. The house was built around 1730 as a country villa (Fig. 19).

The house's furnishings never left and represent the various family generations and their many acquisitions.

The Birthplaces are referred to as "typical New England saltbox structures," built around 1681.

Activities

Guided tours are given at both sites, where you can learn much about the lifestyles of our second and sixth presidents.

JOHN F. KENNEDY NATIONAL HISTORIC SITE

The site is in Brookline, Massachusetts.

Features

The site has the house where JFK was born and lived for four years.

Activities

After touring the house, open from 10:00 A.M. to 4:00 P.M., walk to the Naples Rd. residence where the Kennedy family lived for seven years. The house is not open to the public. However, the school he attended, Edward Devotion School, dates back to the early 1700s and is open to the public Wednesday 2:00 to 4:00 P.M. or by appointment.

Fig. 19. The "Old House" at Quincy Adams House National Historic Site. (National Park Service Photo by Richard Frear)

Information

Superintendent
Adams National Historic Site
P.O. Box 531
Quincy, MA 02269
617-773-1177

LOWELL NATIONAL HISTORICAL PARK

The park is in Lowell, northwest of Boston.

Access

By car, take either Interstate 495 or Route 3 to "Lowell Connector." Stay on Connector to Exit 5N "Thorndike St." and follow signs to park.

Airports

Tew Mac, New York Sectional
Latitude: 42–36
Longitude: 71–12
FSS: 800-242-2377
Car Rentals:
    Hallisy: 617-454-4729

Approximately 10 miles from the site.
Lawrence Municipal, New York Sectional
Latitude: 42–43
Longitude: 71–07
FSS: 800-242-2377
Car Rentals:
    Mr. Rent A Car: 617-682-4111
    Hertz: 617-682-7733
Area rental cars: Agency Rent-A-Car: 617-459-3533
    Mr. Rent A Car: 617-454-0760
    Auto Rent: 617-454-5000

Accommodations

Holiday Inn, restaurant, limo service: 617-851-7301
Merrimack Motor Inn: 617-688-1851
Heritage Inn/Quality Inn, restaurant: 617-256-0800
    or 800-228-5151
Westport Regency, restaurant: 617-692-4123 or 8200

Stay in a historic house, circa 1843:
    Commonwealth House: 617-454-5663
    Camping: Wyman's Beach or in Harold Parker
State Forest

Features

The park preserves Lowell's role in the American Industrial Revolution. In 1810, Francis Cabot Lowell designed the first functioning power loom. The park includes several local parks, including Lowell Heritage State Park. Also in the area are over 5 miles of canals, operating gatehouses, mill worker housing, and 19th-century community structures.

A mill complex, one of the city's first textile corporations, has been restored.

Activities

Stop at the visitors center and see "Lowell, the Industrial Revelation."

See the waterpower exhibit in the Lowell Heritage State Park.

Take a free guided walking tour. Watch performance of "Tunes and Tales" presented three times weekly. Attend a performance of the Merrimack Repertory group in Liberty Hall.

From Memorial Day to Columbus Day, take a 2½ hour Mill and Canal Tour on trolley, barge, and foot (Fig. 20). Reservations: 617-459-1000.

Take a free evening excursion Saturday or Sunday June 19 to August 31 on the Merrimac River departing from the Bellegarde Boathouse. For reservations, call 617-459-1000.

See the Grand Locks and Francis Little Gate,

Fig. 20. Lowell National Historical Park, trolley on Pawtucket Canal. (Photo by James Higgins)

which saved the town from two major floods. Tour reservations required. The tour leaves at quarter past the hour, March 25 to October 14.

Attend a variety of ethnic festivals during the summer months and attend outdoor concerts of the Market Mills Summer Stage.

Enjoy hiking or biking along the Merrimack River, or take a knapsack tour of Lowell during the evening.

Take a free 1-mile ride on the Lowell Park Trolley July and August on Fridays at 6:00 P.M. Call headquarters for reservations.

Visit the historic cemeteries. Some visitors enjoy doing gravestone rubbings here.

Watch the annual Tour de Lowell Bike Race in the summer. Check with the Chamber of Commerce for dates: 617-454-5633.

Tour Whistler House and see etchings and birthplace of American painter James McNeil Whistler.

Information

Superintendent
Lowell National Historical Park
169 Merrimac St.
Lowell, MA 01852
617-459-1000

MINUTE MAN NATIONAL HISTORICAL PARK

The park covers land in Lexington, Lincoln, and Concord.

Airport

Laurence G. Hanscom, New York Sectional
Latitude: 42–28
Longitude: 71–17
FSS: 800-242-2377
Car rentals

Accommodations

In Lexington:
Catch Penny Inn: 617-861-0850
Battle Green Motor Inn: 800-343-0235
(outside MA) or
617-862-6100

Sheraton-Lexington Inn, restaurant:
617-862-8700 or 800-325-3535

In Concord:
Colonial Inn: 617-369-9200
Concordian Motel: 617-263-7765
Howard Johnsons: 617-369-6100

Features

The park commemorates the scenes and events of the conflict of April 19, 1775, which marked the beginning of the Revolutionary War.

Activities

In Concord, tour the North Bridge Visitor Center, 1 mile north of town. Cross the reconstructed bridge and see monuments marking the spot where "the embattled farmers stood and fired the shot heard 'round the world." The Americans had proven they were prepared to fight for their freedom. For information, call 617-369-6993.

Stop by the Wayside at 455 Lexington Road, Concord, to see the historic home of the Alcotts and Hawthornes. Half-hour tours mid-April to October, Friday through Tuesday, 9:30 A.M. to 5:30 P.M.

Visit the restored 18th century Hartwell Tavern June through August from 8:30 A.M. to 5:00 P.M..

Drive Battle Road, which follows almost the same route where the most bitter fighting occurred.

The Concord Antiquarium Museum has 15 period rooms with household furnishings from Concord area homes; 45-minute guided tours available: 617-369-2236.

The Grand Meadows National Wildlife Refuge marsh and upland habitat has good hiking trails.

In Lexington, stop by the visitors center to see a diorama of the clash on the Green.

In Lincoln, stop at the Drumlin Farm to see a working farm and attend a natural historic program. Take a Sunday hayride from 1:00 to 3:00 P.M.: 617-259-9500.

In Sudbury, visit the seventeenth-century Wayside Inn for a meal and tour their period rooms. Its gristmill is open from April to November.

SALEM MARITIME
NATIONAL HISTORIC SITE

The site is located on the waterfront in Salem, and is composed of 9 acres of wharves, grounds, and historic structures.

Airport

Beverly Municipal, New York Sectional
Latitude: 42–35
Longitude: 70–55
FSS: 800-926-3550
Transportation from the airport: North Shore Shuttle Service. Reservations: 617-631-8660
Car rentals:
    Budget: 617-777-3833
The airport is approximately 6 miles from Salem's Historic Site.

Accommodations

Coach House Inn: 617-744-4092
Hawthorne Inn, restaurant, 617-744-4080
Howard Johnsons Motor Lodge, 617-774-8045

Bed and Breakfast: Turner Inn: 617-745-2156

Camping: Near Gloucester, Middleton, Salisbury, Amesbury, North Andover, and Salisbury Beach State Reservation.

Features

In 1790, Salem was the sixth largest city in the U.S. and was a very busy seaport. Imports arrived from the West Indies, China, Indonesia and Arabia. As a result, Elias Derby became the first millionaire in the U.S. His home is near Derby Wharf, where his ships docked.

Salem served as capital of the Massachusetts Bay Colony until 1630. When the witchcraft trials were held, 19 people were hanged and 1 was pressed to death.

Activities

Ride the trolley to get an overall picture of Salem.

The town has houses dating back to the 1680s. Tour the House of Seven Gables made famous by Hawthorne in his book *The Scarlet Letter.*

Visit Pickering Wharf and tour Derby House, home of America's first millionaire.

Visit the Charter Street Burying Ground, where many well-known Salem citizens are buried.

The Witch Dungeon Museum has live presentations of the witch trials. You can also tour the recreated dungeon.

For a chilling reenactment of the witch trials, go to the Salem Witch Museum to see a multimedia sight and sound show, 10:00 A.M. to 5:00 P.M.

The courthouse on Washington and Federal Streets has an exhibit of the pins which the so-called witches used to torment their victims.

Information

Superintendent
Salem Maritime National Historic Site
Custom House, Derby St.
Salem, MA, 01970
617-744-4323

Father Marquette National Memorial

Old Ft. Mackinac •

Michigan

FATHER MARQUETTE NATIONAL MEMORIAL AND MUSEUM

The memorial is in St. Ignace, ¼ mile west of the bridge via Exit 2W.

Airport

Mackinac County, Lake Huron Sectional
Latitude: 45–53
Longitude: 84–44
FSS: 616-539-8401
Taxi

Accommodations

Heritage Inn: 906-643-7581
Captain's Inn: 906-643-9195
Georgian House-Motel: 906-643-8411 or
    800-528-1234

Features

The memorial commemorates the life and work of French Jesuit explorer Father Marquette, who founded the town with his mission.

Activities

Watch programs telling about Father Marquette's life. Hike along the trails.

Visit Castle Rock, 4 miles to the north, to learn about the Algonquin Indians. Open late May through mid-October. 906-643-8266

Information

Superintendent
Father Marquette National Memorial
Straits State Park
720 Church St.
St. Ignace, MI, 49781
906-643-8620

OLD FORT MACKINAC

The fort is on Mackinac Island.

Airport

Mackinac Island, Lake Huron Sectional
Latitude: 45–52
Longitude: 84–38
FSS: 616-539-8401

Accommodations

Grand Hotel: 616-847-3331
Iriquois Hotel: 616-847-3321
The Island House: 616-847-3347

Season

The season runs from mid-April through mid-October. Most accommodations offer a 25 percent discount before June 1 and after September 1.

Features

The fort was built in 1779 above the harbor and is now preserved as a museum. All 14 of the buildings are original, and history is presented through dioramas. Costumed guides are available for hourly tours.

Mackinac Island was the summer playground for the wealthy in the 1800s and has some beautiful Victorian mansions.

Activities

Tours of the fort are conducted hourly, and demonstrate cannon and musket firing.

No automobiles are allowed on the island, making it a bicyclist's heaven. You can rent your own to pedal around the 8½-mile perimeter, or cycle along some of the interior trails. Participate in a cycling race around the island during the summer.

Horses and carriages are also available for a 1½-hour guided tour, or rent your own horse and buggy to ride through the woods.

Visit or stay in the Grand Hotel. A "gawker's fee" is charged for tourists who just want to look around the 660-foot veranda.

Pick up the guidebook for the island (published by the Mackinac Island State Park Commission) to learn more about where to bike and hike.

Information

Mackinac Island Chamber of Commerce
Mackinac Island, MI 49757
906-847-3783 or 906-847-3761

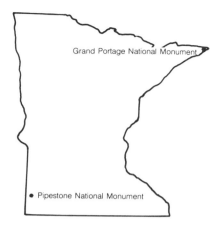

Grand Portage National Monument

Pipestone National Monument

Minnesota

GRAND PORTAGE NATIONAL MONUMENT
The monument is at the northeast end of Minnesota by Lake Superior.

Airport

Devils Track Municipal, Green Bay Sectional
Latitude: 47–49
Longitude: 90–23
FSS: 218-262-3826
You can land both wheeled aircraft and seaplanes.

Full lodging, meals and cabins are available at the lodge located at the strip:
Skyport Lodge: 218-387-1411.
Rental cars in Grand Marais:
Froberg Ford: 218-387-1805

Accommodations

Grand Portage Lodge (closest to monument):
218-476-2401

In Grand Marais:
Allen's Hilltop Cabins: 218-387-2796
Tomteboda Motel: 218-387-1585 or
800-622-2622
Trailside Motor Court: 218-387-1393
Lakeview Cabins: 218-387-2710

There is no camping within the monument. The nearest state park is Judge Magney State Park. Camping is available in Colvill at the Outpost Campground, Grand Marais at Lamb's Resort and Campground, Grand Marais Recreational Area, Hollow Rock Resort, or at the Gunflint Pines Resort and Campground.

Gunflint Trail Resorts:
Skyport Lodge: 218-387-1411
Trout Lake Resort: 218-387-1330
Gateway-Hungry Jack Lodge: 218-388-9979
Sea Island Lodge: 218-388-2261

Climate

Summer weather on the shore is cooler, windier, and damper than inland.

Features

The area was traversed by French Canadians who paddled their canoes 3,000 miles from Montreal with trade goods intended for the Northwest company posts. These barrel-chested, muscular men could tote two 90-pound packs along the rocky ledges and trails over the "big carry" to Pigeon River.

The trip from Canada took 8 weeks and 120 portages in order to reach Grand Portage Bay. The worst portage was at Grand Portage, since they had to carry their canoes and all their gear over the hills and through the swamps.

Although the Grand Portage was not the longest of the portages made by the French Canadian voyageurs, it was where the Northwest Company maintained its Great Hall and held its annual meetings, starting in 1778; these stopped in 1803 when the Northwest Company moved north to Ft. William to avoid taxation by the Americans.

Activities

Hike the Portage Trail, 8½ miles. It begins from the stockade on Lake Superior and goes to the site of Ft. Charlotte, once a way station for furs arriving from the northwest en route to the stockade at Grand Portage. The voyageurs did this trip in 2½ hours. Be prepared for the same problems they faced 200 years ago: slippery terrain, mud, mosquitoes, and black flies.

Hike ½ mile to the top of Mt. Rose behind the stockade, or hike up Cascade River Trail and see five waterfalls.

Combine hiking with canoeing and follow the ancient portages from lake to lake.

Compete in the summer canoe race on the Gunflint Trail.

Celebrate the reenactment of the annual meeting of the trappers.

Canoe Outfitters:
Bear Track Outfitting Co.: 218-387-1162
O Hungry Jack Outfitters: 218-388-2275
Gunflint Northwoods Outfitters: 800-328-3362
Way of the Wilderness Outfitters: 218-388-2212

Nearby Attraction

Grand Portage is only 22 miles from Isle Royale National Park.

Information

Superintendent
Grand Portage National Monument
P.O. Box 666
Grand Marais, MN 55604
218-387-2788

PIPESTONE NATIONAL MONUMENT

The monument is on the north side of Pipestone in southwest Minnesota.

Airport

Pipestone Municipal, Omaha Sectional
Latitude: 43–59
Longitude: 96–18
FSS: 800-272-1402
Car rentals

Accommodations

Calumet Hotel: 507-825-4273
King Kourt Motel: 507-825-3314
Mayfair Motel: 507-825-3381

Features

To this day, only Indians are permitted to mine the red stone called pipestone catlinite, which they have used to make ceremonial pipes for over three centuries. This rock was formed as a bed of red clay laid down between two layers of sandstone that became the metamorphic rock called quartzite.

Activities

Visit the visitors center. Indian craftsmen work on pipestone during the summer, and pipestone pipes may be purchased at the Upper Midwest Indian Cultural Center.

Follow the self-guided Circle Trail to the quarries, Winnewissa Falls, Lake Hiawatha, and Leaping Rock.

Information

Superintendent
Pipestone National Monument
P.O. Box 727
Pipestone, MN, 56164
507-825-5463

Natchez Trace Parkway ●

● Vicksburg National Military Park

Fort Massachusetts

Mississippi

FORT MASSACHUSETTS

The fort is located on the western end of West Ship Island near Biloxi.

Airport

Gulfport-Biloxi Regional
New Orleans Sectional
Latitude: 30–24
Longitude: 89–04
FSS: 601-436-4384

Accommodations

In Biloxi:
    Best Western Biloxi Inn, restaurant:
      601-388-1000
    Econo Lodge Motel, restaurant: 601-374-7644
    Howard Johnson's Motor Lodge, restaurant:
      601-388-6310

In Gulfport:
    Ramada Inn, restaurant: 601-864-8811
    Best Western Seaway Inn, restaurant, airport

    transportation: 601-864-0050
    Worth Motor Lodge: 601-896-3641

Features

The fort preserves the Civil War era masonry structure. Its construction dates back to 1858. It was occupied by Federal troops who used it as a vital part of the naval blockade bringing defeat to the South.

Activities

Take a free tour. Access is via tour boat from the Port of Gulfport, 12 miles south of Gulfport. The trip takes 70 minutes. For reservations, call 601-436-6010. You can also get to Ship Island from Biloxi, which is 28 miles away.

Tour Beauvoir, the last home of Jefferson Davis. It's located midway between Biloxi and Gulfport on Highway 90. The home was completed in 1852 and Davis lived here 12 years. Tour the East Cottage where Davis had his library and wrote *The Rise and Fall of the Confederate Government*.

NATCHEZ TRACE PARKWAY

The parkway runs from Natchez to Nashville.

Climate

Summer is generally hot and humid. The winter is cold and damp, with occasional warm spells. Spring and autumn weather is mild and warm.

Accommodations

No accommodations are available directly along the parkway, but many are easily found in the nearby towns. Many offer bed and breakfast in beautiful old mansions.

In Natchez: Bed and Breakfast:
  The Burn in Natchez, c. 1832, 601-445-8566
  Anchuca, c. 1830 mansion: 601-636-4931
  Hope Farm, c. 1774, 601-442-5132
  Monmouth Plantation, c. 1818, 601-442-5852

In Tupelo:
  Hilton Inn, 601-841-2222
  Best Western Trace Inn, 601-842-5555
  Ramada Inn, 601-844-4111
  Town House Motel: 601-842-5411

Camping (Note: Campers should be sure to bring along repellent and insect netting): Milepost 227: Camp Sleepy Hollow Campground. Attend the blue grass festival here the third weekend in June and on Labor Day.

There are 16 additional campgrounds along the route including Rocky Springs, Jeff Busby and Meriwether Lewis.

Milepost 317: Tishomingo State Park: Family camping and cabins. For reservations, call 601-438-6914.

Features

Natchez Trace, French for "footpath," is a 450-mile parkway, roughly following the route of the original Natchez Trace through Mississippi, Alabama, and Tennessee, and connecting Natchez, Jackson, Tupelo, and Nashville. The Parkway passes several archeological sites and historical landmarks.

About 8,000 years ago, the path was beaten by buffalo along the watershed. Then it became an old Indian trail well enough defined that early maps drawn in 1733 showed it going from Natchez to Choctaw villages. It was later used by French traders, missionaries, and soldiers.

Around 1785, the Old Trace was made famous by the Ohio Valley settlers called "Kaintucks" who, in the early 1800s, floated down the Mississippi River in flatboats. They sold their boats in Natchez or New Orleans, hid their gold in their boot heels, or sewed it into their breeches. Then, the only way to return home was to walk or ride the 450 miles from Natchez to Nashville.

From 1800 to 1820, the rough road was used by boatmen, soldiers, postmen, missionaries, Indians, and pioneer settlers.

When the steamer *New Orleans* appeared in 1812, it heralded the beginning of steamboats going between the cities. By 1819, 20 steamboats were operating between New Orleans and the interior cities, and the trace reverted back to being a quiet country lane.

Activities

Each spring and fall, many antebellum homes in Natchez are opened for visitation in a celebration known as the Pilgrimage.

Milepost 233.2: Take horseback rides of either 9 or 15 miles from the Witch Dance picnic area.

Bikers can obtain a set of alternate bike routes between Natchez and Nashville from the Eastern National Parks and Monuments Association.

Hiking is available 28 miles along the parkway. There are also 13 nature trails. Trails begin at Rocky Springs Campground, milepost 54.8; at Owens Creek, milepost 52.4; milepost 184: Hike along Bullen Creek through a hardwood forest. Tour Vicksburg National Military Park; Jeff Busby Campground, milepost 193.0; and Meriwether Lewis Campground, milepost 385.9.

Attend the Natchez Pilgrimage held annually each spring and fall. It's one of the oldest and largest festivals held in North America. Attend evening entertainment: Confederate Pageant, Southern Ex-

Fig. 21. Mt. Locust, a restored early 1800 inn or "stand," Natchez Trace Parkway. (National Park Service Photo by W. L. Sigafoos)

posure, Mississippi Medicine Show, and Moonlight and Magnolias show. For information and reservations: P.O. Box 347, Natchez, MS 39120.

North of Natchez you can visit Emerald Mound, built by the ancestors of the Natchez Indians.

In Tupelo, tour the national battlefield site where the Confederate cavalry attacked the Union forces (Fig. 22). The battlefield is within the city limits and 1⅕ miles east of the Natchez Visitors Center.

Also in Tupelo, tour the visitors center where sorghum is made the last weekend in September and every weekend in October. Also hike the nearby nature trail.

Beyond milepost 317, stop in Tishomingo State Park, where you can see an 1840s log cabin and the famous swinging bridge over Bear Creek, take a canoe float trip on Bear Creek, and attend the Bear Creek Folklife Festival the first Saturday in June.

Milepost 341.8: Tuscumbia, Alabama: Visit Ivy Green, birthplace of Helen Keller. Attend a perfor-mance of "The Miracle Worker" on weekends June through July. Reservations: 205-383-4066.

Terminus of the Trace: Nashville, TN: Home of the Grand Ole Opry, Andrew Jackson's "The Hermitage," and other historical homes (Fig. 21).

Information

Natchez Trace Parkway
RR 1, NT-143
Tupelo, MS, 38801
601-842-1572

VICKSBURG NATIONAL MILITARY PARK

The park is located along the Mississippi River near Vicksburg.

Airport

Vicksburg Municipal, Memphis Sectional
Latitude: 32–14

Fig. 22. Tupelo National Battlefield. (National Park Service Photo by Francis Elmore)

Longitude: 90–55
FSS: 601-638-4161
Car rentals: 601-636-2766 or 601-636-4936

Accommodations

Holiday Inn, restaurant: 601-636-4551
Ramada Inn, restaurant: 601-638-5811
Cedar Grove: 601-636-1605

Two antebellum homes offer bed and breakfast: Anchuca 601-636-4931, and Cedar Grove.

Features

Vicksburg controlled the Mississippi, making its capture a vital part of General Grant's strategy to split the Confederacy. The Union forces kept the city under siege, but hunger and a lack of supplies led to their ultimate downfall. On July 4, 1863, the Confederates stacked their arms and marched out.

Activities

The monument forms a semicircular park around the city with memorials and tablets marking the positions of the two armies. A 16-mile road follows the progress of the Union forces with 15 marked stops along the way.

On Fort Hill, the Confederate guns are still trained on the riverbed. A voice box relates the story of the ironclad Union gunboats.

Take the 3-hour Vicksburg Deluxe Tour through the military park, Courthouse Museum, and two antebellum homes. For information, call 601-638-8888 or 800-862-1300.

Visit the Old Courthouse Museum downtown, which contains Southern antebellum artifacts.

Tour the Waterways Experimental Station, the world's largest research testing and developmental facility, operated by the U.S. Army Corps of Engineers. Free.

Information

Superintendent
Vicksburg National Military Park
P.O. Box 110
Vicksburg, MS 39180
800-221-3536

Jefferson National Expansion
Memorial National Historic Site

Missouri

JEFFERSON NATIONAL EXPANSION MEMORIAL NATIONAL HISTORIC SITE

The memorial is on the waterfront at Market Street along the Mississippi River.

Airports

Arrowhead, St. Louis Sectional
Latitude: 38–41
Longitude: 90–31
FSS: 314-532-1011
Taxi

Creve Couer, St. Louis Sectional
Latitude: 38–43
Longitude: 90–30
FSS: 800-392-4220
Car rentals: 314-921-6111

Lambert-St. Louis International, St. Louis Sectional
Latitude: 38–45
Longitude: 90–21
FSS: 800-392-4220
Car rentals:
    Budget: 314-423-3000
    Avis: 314-426-7766
    Hertz: 314-426-7555

Climate

The summers can be warm and humid and briefly very hot. Spring and fall temperatures are more moderate, while winters can be cold.

Accommodations

Downtown:
    Clarion Hotel St. Louis, restaurant, near river: 314-241-9500
    Bel Air Hilton, restaurant, near river: 314-621-7900
    Quality Inn, airport: 314-524-2500

    Bed and Breakfast list of homes: 314-533-9299

Features

The Gateway Arch rises 630 feet above the site of Pierre de Laciede's house and trading post. It commemorates the gateway to the West for thousands of pioneers from the East. Lewis conducted preexploration business here and later served as governor. The expedition returned here in 1806.

William Clark is buried at Clark Gravesite and Monument in Bellefontaine Cemetery. The cemetery also has other notable gravesites.

Activities

Tour the visitors center beneath the Arch and go through the Museum of Westward Expansion. Watch two 30-minute movies on the early pioneers.

Ride the tram to the top of the Arch. Be sure to allow enough time to get your ticket, since the lines tend to be long during tourist season. Tickets may only be purchased on the day you intend to ride.

Pick up a self-guided tour map at the Gateway Arch of the historic section of the city.

Additional Features

Tour the Missouri Botanical Gardens at 4344 Shaw Boulevard. It's a National Historic Landmark and one of the world's largest, containing nine separate gardens within its boundary. Take a guided tour through Tower Grove House, home of Henry Shaw, founder of the garden. Watch a film in the center's orientation theater. Electric trams offer 20-minute tours of the gardens, or you can rent a cassette to take a walking tour. Open 9:00 A.M. to 7:30 P.M.

Take a cruise on the Mississippi aboard the Huck Finn and Tom Sawyer Cruise ships: 314-621-4040. Watch the annual Memorial Day Riverboat race: 314-421-1023

Watch the Great Meramek River Raft Race and Festival in late June. Homemade rafts make a 4½-mile float down the river: 314-889-2863.

Tour the Anheuser-Busch Brewery at Broad-way and Pestalozzi and see not only the brewhouse but the Clydesdale stables. Pick up a complimentary sample: 314-577-2626.

Tour the McDonnell Douglas Prologue Room and aerospace museum. It has a fascinating display for pilots. Open Monday through Saturday 9:00 A.M. to 4:00 P.M., June through August. The St. Louis Science Center houses the McDonnell Planetarium. For information, call 314-652-5500.

The Old Courthouse at 11 N. Fourth St. was the setting of the Dred Scott case. One-hour guided tours are available, and informational films are shown.

The National Museum of Transport, 16 miles west of the city, has a large display of vehicles from horse-drawn buggies to vintage aircraft. Call 314-231-6340.

Attend the Annual National Ragtime and Traditional Jazz Festival in mid-June. Call 314-621-3311.

The Great Forest Park Balloon Race occurs in mid-September. Call 314-726-6896.

Information

Superintendent
Jefferson National Expansion Memorial
National Historic Site
11 N. 4th St.
St. Louis, MO 63102
314-425-4465

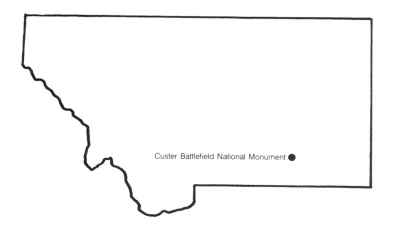

Montana

CUSTER BATTLEFIELD NATIONAL MONUMENT

The monument is 15 miles south of Hardin. From Billings, go southeast on Highway 212.

Airports

Hardin-Fairgrounds, Billings Sectional
Latitude: 45–43
Longitude: 107–36
FSS: 406-259-4545
Car rentals available:
  Triangle Motors: 406-665-2104
  Hardin Auto: 406-665-1211

Wisdom, Great Falls Sectional
Latitude: 45–35
Longitude: 113–27
FSS: 406-388-4242
No car rentals. 10 miles from the monument.

Butte, Bert Mooney Field, Great Falls Sectional
Latitude: 45–57
Longitude: 112–30
FSS: 406-494-3004
Car rentals; 85 miles from the monument.

Accommodations

In Billings:
  Best Western Northern Hotel: 406-245-5121
  Lewis and Clark Inn: 800-541-9312 (outside MT)
  Kings Rest Motel: 406-252-8451

In Hardin:
  Western Motel: 406-665-2296
  Lariat Motel: 406-665-2683
  American Inn of Hardin: 406-665-1870

Features

The area covers $1\frac{1}{5}$ square miles and has a memorial honoring the climax of the Indian Wars (Fig. 23). It also preserves the site of the last great victory for the Indians, who were fighting to preserve the ancestral way of life. When gold was discovered in the Black Hills in 1874, it brought prospectors into the region in complete violation of the Ft. Laramie Treaty.

Here, in June 1876, Gen. Custer and 225 men of the 7th Cavalry Regiment made their last stand against several thousand Sioux and Cheyenne.

Fig. 23. Aerial of Custer Battlefield.

Custer's headstone and military gravesite are located here. Comanche, a pet horse, survived the slaughter, and was stuffed following his death.

Activities

Guided battlefield walks of 30 to 45 minutes are offered. Also take a guided national cemetery walk of 15 to 20 minutes, or drive through the grounds on Battlefield Road. A 30-minute movie is also available at the visitors center.

The battlefield tour begins at the Reno-Benteen site, 4½ miles from the visitors center. If you go up Custer Hill, you can see most of the battlefield and the valley where the Indian village under Sioux Chief Sitting Bull was encamped.

Hike the ½-mile loop trail to the bluffs overlooking Little Bighorn Valley.

Nearby Attraction

Custer National Forest has the Absaroka-Beartooth Wilderness Area and the highest point in Montana: Granite Peak at 12,799 feet. Drive along Beartooth Scenic Highway from Memorial Day through September 30, and enjoy hiking along the trails.

Big Horn National Recreation Area is open from Memorial Day to September 30.

Information

Superintendent
Custer Battlefield National Monument
P.O. Box 39
Crow Agency, MT 59022
406-638-2622

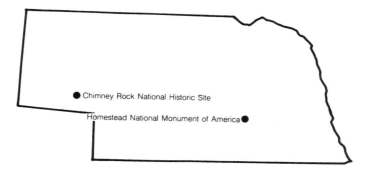

Nebraska

CHIMNEY ROCK NATIONAL HISTORIC SITE

The site is 23 miles east of Scotts Bluff National Monument.

Airport

Scottsbluff County, Cheyenne Sectional
Latitude: 41–52
Longitude: 103–3
FSS: 800-682-5122
Car rentals

Lincoln Municipal, Omaha Sectional
Latitude: 40–51
Longitude: 96–45
FSS: 800-742-7705
Car rentals

Accommodations

In Scottsbluff:
    Friendship Inn: Sands Motel: 308-632-6191
    Candlelight Inn: 308-635-3751
    Best Western Lamplighter Motel: 308-632-7108

In Lincoln:
    Harvester Motel: 402-423-3131
    Best Western Villager Motor Inn: 402-464-9111
    Great Plains Motel: 402-476-3253

Features

Chimney Rock is a slender rock column that is apart from the ridge that forms the North Platte Valley. It's formed of clay with layers of volcanic ash and sandstone.

The "Rock" is located along one of the most popular migration corridors to be followed in American history. Many well-known names passed by here including Lewis and Clark, Smith, Jackson, and Sublette in 1830, and Brigham Young in 1847. In 1843, one of the first emigrant wagon trains passed by here, led by Bidwell.

During the California gold rush, it's estimated that approximately 250,000 gold-seekers came by here in their covered wagons. By the mid 1850s to the 1860s, this route was traveled more by military personnel and ox-drawn freighters. Later, the cavalry was replaced by homesteaders, who arrived here in 1884.

The route's most popular name was "The Oregon Trail," which began in Missouri, and led settlers to the west. Chimney Rock is probably one of the best-known landmarks they knew. Many climbed its tower, leaving their signatures behind, but the clay wasn't strong enough to keep them for us to read.

Activities

The best way to see this famous landmark is from the air, since the ground access is via gravel roads, with the last part via a rough foot trail. If interested, you can see some mobile trailer exhibits along Nebraska 92, or in Scotts Bluff National Monument.

Information

Superintendent
Chimney Rock National Historic Site
Bayard, NE 68508
308-586-2022

HOMESTEAD NATIONAL MONUMENT OF AMERICA

The monument is 4½ miles west of Beatrice.

Airport

Beatrice Municipal, Omaha Sectional
Latitude: 40–18
Longitude: 96–45
FSS: 800-742-7705
Car rentals: Burnham Motors: 402-223-3547.

Accommodations

In Beatrice:
    Best Western Inn: 402-223-4074
    Holiday Villa Motel: 402-223-4036
    Super 8 Motel: 402-223-3536

Camping is available in and around Beatrice in six parks, including Rockford Lake, 8 miles east. Both Rockford and Big Indian Recreation Area, 15 miles south of town, offer water activities and hiking.

Features

The monument was established to commemorate the Homestead Act of 1862 as well as the

Fig. 24. The Palmer-Epard Cabin at Homestead National Monument is on the claim of Daniel Freeman, one of the first pioneers to file for free land under the Homestead Act of 1862. (National Park Service Photo)

contributions of the early pioneers. Daniel Freeman staked out the land in 1862, becoming the first homesteader in the United States.

At first, these homesteaders had to build their houses, live on the land, and cultivate it for 5 years. Then, after the Civil War, thousands of veterans, European immigrants, and black families, many ex-slaves, came west to take advantage of the availability of free land. Population in Kansas, Nebraska, the Dakotas, and Montana soared.

Activities

Tour the visitors center and museum. See an authentic nineteenth-century settler's cabin, one-room schoolhouse, and implements from life on the early frontier. The school wasn't only important for the children's education, but also served as the focal point for many of the settlers' social and religious activities. It's open from March through November (Fig. 24).

You can also see living history displays of cooking and farming.

Hike along a 2⅖-kilometer self-guided trail that takes you past some of the major points of interest along the original homestead site situated in a tall grass prairie. As you look at the Palmer-Epard Cabin built in 1867, can you imagine what it must have been like to raise a family here?

During the last week in June, attend "Homestead Days," a 5-day event in which you can watch local volunteers demonstrate the crafts of the 1800s. There's also a parade and other special programs. For information: 402-223-2338.

In mid-December, visit the Homestead to enjoy Christmas celebrations as they were observed in the late 1800s.

Nearby Attraction

In Bellevue, tour the Strategic Air Command Museum and see a collection of military aircraft located next to the nation's defense "nerve center." It's open year-round 8:00 A.M. to 5:00 P.M. daily.

Information

Superintendent
Homestead National Monument
Rte. 3, Box 47
Beatrice, NE 68310
402-223-3514

Nevada

Virginia City National Historic Landmark

VIRGINIA CITY NATIONAL HISTORIC LANDMARK

Airports

Reno/Stead, San Francisco Sectional
Latitude: 39–40
Longitude: 119–53
FSS: 702-785-3000
Bus transportation to Reno.
Car rentals in Reno:
    Alamo Rent-a-Car: 800-327-9633
    Avis: 800-331-1212
    Budget: 702-785-2541

Reno Cannon International, San Francisco Sectional
Latitude: 39–30
Longitude: 119–46
FSS: 702-785-3000
Car rentals

Accommodations

In Reno:
    River Houses Motor Hotel: 702-329-0036
    Sierra Street Inn: 702-322-2106
    Thunderbird Motel: 702-329-3578

In Virginia City:
    The Castle: 702-847-0275
    Mackay Mansion: 702-847-0173
    Savage Mansion: 702-847-0574
    Comstock Motel: 702-847-0233

In Tahoe:
    All Seasons Resort: 702-831-2311
    Hyatt Lake Tahoe: 702-831-1111 or 800-228-9000
    Incline Motor Lodge: 702-831-1052

Camping is available in Carson City, Lake Tahoe and in Reno.

Features

The town began in 1859, and became the richest mining town in the world. The Civil War was partially financed from its silver and gold.

In the 1870s, Virginia City had 30,000 residents, 110 saloons, and the only elevator to be found between Chicago and San Francisco. The Comstock Lode was one of the richest gold and silver deposits to be found, with approximately $234 million in ore mined.

Activities

Visit some of the museums along C Street, and take an underground mine tour offered every 20 minutes by the Ponderosa Saloon.

Stop by the Visitors Bureau on C Street to watch a short historical film. Call 702-847-0177 for the schedule.

The annual Camel Races occur the second weekend in September, commemorating the animals used to help the cavalry and to carry salt to the mines. The Ferrari Hill Climb is also held in September. For information, call: 847-0311.

Tour the castle built in 1868 for mining baron Robert Graves.

Go through the Mark Twain Museum and listen to some of his stories.

Take a 25-minute trail ride from Virginia City to Gold City aboard the Virginia and Truckee Railroad.

Attend the Piper's Opera House Sunday concerts in July.

In nearby Carson City, attend the Soaring National Championships in July, or in mid-June, attend the Wagon Train Weekend commemorating the route taken by the early settlers.

While in Reno, "the biggest little city in the world," tour Harrah's Automobile Collection and see many classic cars plus a few antique airplanes. Harrah's offers free shuttle bus transportation from the Hotel/Casino. Reno also has the National Championship Air Races (Fig. 25) at Stead Air Field in mid-September: 702-826-7500.

Nearby Lake Tahoe offers golfing, water sports, sternwheeler cruises, and a tram ride. In May, watch the Great Lake Tahoe Sternwheeler Race. July offers a summer music festival, and August has a Shakespeare Festival. October features a Dixieland Jazz Festival.

Information

Storey County Chamber of Commerce
P.O. Box 474
Virginia City, NV 89440

Fig. 25. Reno Air Races. (courtesy Reno Chamber of Commerce)

New Hampshire

Saint-Gaudens
National Historic Site

SAINT-GAUDENS NATIONAL HISTORIC SITE

The site is located off New Hampshire State Route 12-A in Cornish, New Hampshire. It's 9 miles north of Claremont, New Hampshire, or 2 miles from Windsor, Vermont. Take the Ascutney or Hartland, Vermont, exit if driving Interstate 91. If you're driving on Interstate 89, take the West Lebanon, New Hampshire, exit.

Airport

Lebanon Regional Airport, New York Sectional
Latitude: 43–37
Longitude: 72–18
FSS: 603-298-8360
Car rentals available in town.

Season

The site is open daily beginning with the last weekend in May through the end of October. The buildings open at 8:30 A.M. and close at 4:30 P.M. The grounds are open from 8:00 A.M. until dark.

Accommodations

Old Newfane Inn: 802-365-4427

Inn at Mt. Ascutney: 603-484-7725
Quechee Inn at Marshland Farm, a circa 1793 farm-house: 603-395-3133
The Lyme Inn, Lyme, NH: 603-795-2222
Rabbit Hill Motor Inn, Waterford, VT: 802-748-5168

Features

Augustus Saint-Gaudens lived from 1848 to 1907, and was one of America's greatest sculptors. The site was his summer residence from 1885 to 1897, and it later became his permanent residence from 1900 until he died in 1907.

You can tour his house, which contains the original furnishings. He also loved gardening, and you can walk through his formal gardens and see the old bowling green where he and his friends enjoyed lawn bowling. As you stroll about the grounds, you can see over 100 pieces of his work, including a copy of Adams Memorial, one of his most famous works.

Activities

Take the Ravine Trail, which begins at the Ravine Studio. This ¼-mile trail follows an old cart path often visited by the sculptor and takes you to the Temple, where you can follow 2½-mile Blow-Me-Down trail.

Nearby Attractions

Tour Dartmouth campus or attend a concert or play at Hopkins Center of the Arts in Hanover. For information, call 603-646-2422.

Fish in the Connecticut River for northern pike, bass, perch, and pickerel. You can also boat, kayak, or canoe on the river.

Tour the birthplace of Calvin Coolidge in Plymouth, or see five covered bridges located in Cornish and Plainfield.

To do some bicycling, obtain maps from the New Hampshire Department of Resource and Economic Development Office of Recreation Services and Office of Vacation Travel, P.O. Box 856, Concord, NH, 03301.

Information

Saint-Gaudens National Historic Site
RR 2
Cornish, NH 03745
603-675-2175

Morristown National Historical Park ● ● Edison National Historic Site

New Jersey

EDISON NATIONAL HISTORIC SITE

This site is about 30 minutes away by car from Morristown. The headquarters are on Main Street at Lakeside Avenue in West Orange, 2 miles west of Garden State Parkway and ½ mile north of I-280.

Airport

Morristown Municipal, New York Sectional
Latitude: 40–47
Longitude: 74–24
FSS: 800-932-0835
Car rentals available:
    201-538-6400, or Elegant Car Service: 201-993-5995
    In town: Morristown Lincoln Mercury: 201-538-6373
The airport is 3 miles east of Morristown.

Accommodations

In West Orange:
    Turtle Brook Inn: 201-731-5300

In East Hanover:
    Holiday Inn: 201-994-3500
    Roadway Inn: 201-887-9300

In East Orange:
    Royal Inn: 201-677-3100

Features

Thomas Edison was awarded 1,093 patents in his lifetime, the highest number of patents ever granted to any one person. He built a lab here that was designed to be the ultimate research laboratory. His lab employed a staff of about 60 people, and Edison stocked his labs with every possible substance they might need in their research—or, as Edison once remarked, ''Everything from an elephant's hide to the eyeballs of a U.S. Senator.''

The West Orange labs remained in operation until Edison's death in 1931. Today the Bell labs and the Westinghouse labs have been patterned after Edison's lab.

Activities

Take a guided tour of the lab and see many of the original inventions on display. The tours last

1½ hours and are conducted daily beginning at 9:30 A.M. The last tour departs at 3:00 P.M. You can also attend a showing of one of Edison's early movies.

Tour Glenmont, Edison's beautiful home that he shared with Mina Miller, daughter of a wealthy midwestern manufacturer. Tours of the house begin on the hour from 12:00 to 4:00 P.M. Wednesdays through Sundays, except holidays, by making prior arrangements at headquarters.

Information

Park Manager
Edison National Historic Site
Main St. at Lakeside Ave.
West Orange, NJ 07052
201-736-5050

MORRISTOWN NATIONAL HISTORICAL PARK

The park is in Morristown.

Airport

Morristown Municipal, New York Sectional
Latitude: 40–47
Longitude: 74–24
FSS: 800-932-0835
Car rentals:
    201-538-6400
    Elegant Car Service: 201-993-5995
    In town: Morristown Lincoln Mercury: 201-538-6373
The airport is 3 miles east of Morristown.

Accommodations

In Morristown:
    Governor Morris Inn: 201-539-7300
    Morristown Motor Inn: 201-540-1700
    Holiday Inn: 201-994-3500
    Rodeway Inn: 201-887-9300

Camping: Broomwood Lakes Club or Mahlon Dickerson Reservation: 201-829-8373. Obtain permit at Morristown police station. There are six additional campgrounds in the surrounding state parks.

Season

Headquarters and museum are open daily 9:00 A.M. to 5:00 P.M. Park roads are open from 9:00 A.M. until sunset. The park may occasionally be closed by snow or other hazardous driving conditions.

Features

In 1777, and again during the winter of 1779–80, Washington established his Continental army winter quarters here. He brought 10,000 men, and as the winter wore on, had to overcome desertion and disease in his efforts to build an army capable of fighting against William Howe's Redcoats.

The winter of 1779 proved to be one of the most severe on record when the area was hit with 28 blizzards. Washington established his own headquarters in the home of Jacob Ford, Jr., while his men built their own barracks. By January 1780, the soldiers had constructed almost 1,200 huts in Jockey Hollow, making the area temporarily the sixth largest city in the United States.

In May, France sent six warships and 6,000 French soldiers to assist in the Americans' efforts. Washington ordered his troops from Morristown, ending the encampment.

Activities

The park has three units: Washington's Headquarters located in Morristown (Fig. 26), which can be toured; Ft. Nonsense, and Jockey Hollow. In the Hollow area, you can hike along 27 miles of trails and stop at the visitors center for a movie.

Information

Superintendent
Morristown National Historical Park
Washington Place
Morristown, NJ 07960
201-539-2016

Fig. 26. Morristown National Historical Park. (National Park Service Photo by Richard Frear)

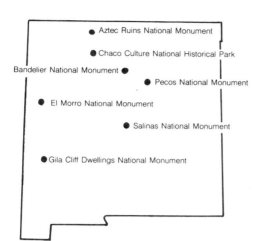

- Aztec Ruins National Monument
- Chaco Culture National Historical Park
- Bandelier National Monument
- Pecos National Monument
- El Morro National Monument
- Salinas National Monument
- Gila Cliff Dwellings National Monument

New Mexico

AZTEC RUINS NATIONAL MONUMENT

The ruins are located 1 mile northwest of Aztec and 14 miles northwest of Farmington.

Airports

Aztec Municipal, Denver Sectional
Latitude: 36–50
Longitude: 108–01
FSS: 505-722-4308

Farmington Municipal, Denver Sectional
Latitude: 36–44
Longitude: 108–13
FSS: 505-722-4308
Car rentals
The airport is 14 miles from the monument.

Climate

Summer highs are in the 90s with lows in the 40s and 50s. Expect evening thunderstorms late in the summer. Fall and spring temperatures range between 40° F and 80° F. Spring weather is windy. Winter temperatures range between 20° F and 40° F, but little snow is received.

Accommodations

No accommodations are available in the monument.

In Aztec:
Enchantment Lodge: 505-334-6143
Best Western: 505-334-2828

In Farmington:
The Basin Lodge: 505-325-5061
Best Western, restaurant: 505-327-5221
Holiday Inn, restaurant: 505-327-9811

Features

The ruins were named by early American settlers, who assumed that the ancient builders were Aztecs. The ruins contain one of the largest pre-Spanish towns in the southwest, and were occupied from 1100 to 1300.

The large three-story and 50-room pueblo's architecture combines the features of both the Chaco and Mesa Verde Indians. The community was built around a central plaza containing a huge kiva, or ceremonial lodge. This kiva represents the only restoration of its kind in North America. The area was abandoned in the thirteenth or fourteenth century.

Activities

The visitors center contains a series of indoor and outdoor exhibits. Guided tours are also available upon request.

A ¼-mile self-guiding trail winds through the pueblo, the great kiva, and the Hubbard Ruin, a triwalled structure.

Additional Attractions

Visit Navajo Lake, 23 miles east of Aztec. It's New Mexico's largest lake and offers good fishing, water skiing, boating, and camping.

Salmon Ruins are 12 miles from Aztec. The Salmon Pueblo is one of the largest colonies founded by the Chacoans in the eleventh century.

Kutz Canyon and Angel Peak Recreation Area is 24 miles south of Aztec. Drive along Canyon Rim Drive to get an overlook of the Grand Canyon.

Information

Superintendent
P.O. Box 4
Aztec, NM 87410
505-334-6174

BANDELIER NATIONAL MONUMENT

Bandelier is 46 miles west of Santa Fe. It has two approaches. You can drive north from Santa Fe on US 285 to Pojoaque, and then west on NM 4. If the weather and road conditions are good, you can drive through the Jemez Mountains from Albuquerque.

Airports

Santa Fe County Municipal, Albuquerque Sectional
Latitude: 35–3
Longitude: 106–05
FSS: 505-982-3871
Car rentals

Albuquerque-Alameda, Albuquerque Sectional
Latitude: 35–11
Longitude: 106–40
FSS: 505-243-7831
Car rentals

Albuquerque-Coronado, Albuquerque Sectional
Latitude: 35–11
Longitude: 106–34
FSS: 505-243-7831
Car rentals

Climate

From May through December, temperatures range from the 80s during the day to the 50s at night, with low relative humidity. Thunderstorms are common in July and August.

Accommodations

Frijoles Canyon Lodge is open during the summer:
    505-672-9791

In Los Alamos (closest town to the monument):
    Los Alamos Inn, restaurant: 505-662-7211
    Hilltop House: 505-662-2441
    Los Alamos Inn: 505-662-7211
    Los Alamos Bed and Breakfast: 505-662-6041
    Orange Street Bed and Breakfast: 505-662-2651

In White Rock:
    White Rock Motor Lodge: 505-672-3838

Camping: Juniper Campground is located near the entrance. Call 505-672-3861. A snack shop is open during the summer.

Features

The monument features some manmade cave rooms carved in the cliffs. The Indians farmed this area seven to eight centuries ago and lived in the cave rooms, on the canyon floor, and along the mesa top. The most accessible rooms were cut out of soft tuff rock. Some houses were built on the talus slopes.

The visitors center on the north side has a lunch area. Its museum traces the Indian culture from 1200 A.D. to the present.

When approaching the area, you drop down 500 feet into Frijole Canyon from the Pajarito Plateau, located on the rim of one of the world's greatest calderas, a huge bowl created by the collapse of the summit of a volcano. The Jemez Mountains contain basaltic lava from the old volcano.

Activities

Most of Bandelier has been designated a wilderness area and is only accessible via 60 miles of maintained trails. All backcountry hikers should be registered and wilderness permits obtained.

One of the most popular hikes is from Upper Frijoles Crossing downstream to the monument headquarters. Other trails go to Alamo Canyon, 3 miles one way; Stone Lions, 6 miles; Painted Cave, 9⅗ miles; Capulin Canyon's bottom, 7 miles; Upper Crossing, 5⅗ miles; and to the pueblo ruins of San Miguel-Yapashi.

Follow the self-guided trail to see where fourteenth century Pueblo Indians excavated cliff dwellings in the volcanic rock forming the canyon walls. Their only cutting tools were harder stones.

For additional trail information, see *A Guide to Bandelier Monument* by Dorothy Hoard.

Climb the ladders to see indentations that once anchored ancient looms. Also watch for a petroglyph of a parrot painted on the sheer rock.

Tsankawi is in a separate section of the monument and has a large, unexcavated, mesa-top pueblo ruin. It's only accessible via the partially original 2-mile self-guided trail. To tour this ruin requires approximately 1½ hours.

Nearby Attractions

Tour the Los Alamos National Lab, where the world's first nuclear weapons were developed. See their exhibits showing the latest research in solar and geothermal energy.

In Santa Fe, attend the Santa Fe Opera, which features some of the world's best musical talent. The season runs from the latter part of June through the last week in August. Five productions are presented in rotation, so you can enjoy several different shows over a stay of a few days.

During most of July, performances are given on Wednesday, Friday and Saturday evenings. Beginning the last week of July, the opera goes six nights a week on a Monday to Saturday schedule. Information: Opera Association of New Mexico, P.O. Box 2408, Santa Fe, NM 87501, or call 505-982-3851.

The city is also known for its artisans and Indian and Spanish cultures. Over 3,000 artists live here year-round.

Information

Superintendent
Los Alamos, NM 87544
505-672-3861

CHACO CULTURE NATIONAL HISTORICAL PARK

The closest town to Chaco is Crownpoint, 100 miles west of Albuquerque. To drive to the area from the north, turn south at Blanco Trading Post on New Mexico 44, which is paved, to New Mexico 57 (unpaved) and drive for 23 miles.

If you are arriving by car from the south, turn north from Interstate 40 at Thoreau onto New Mexico 57, passing Crownpoint, and then turn north to go 20 miles on NM 57 (unpaved from this point on) to the south entrance.

This monument is located in a canyon 41 miles from the nearest town and 20 miles from the paved road, along a road that is often impassable after a snowstorm or thundershower.

Airport

Farmington Municipal, Denver Sectional
Latitude: 36–44
Longitude: 108–13
FSS: 505-722-4308
Car rentals.

The airport is approximately 60 miles from Chaco.

Accommodations

There are no services between Blanco Trading Post and Crownpoint. There is no gas, food, or lodging available in the monument.

In Farmington:
Basin Lodge: 505-753-7291
La Quinta Motor Inn: 505-527-4706
Holiday Inn: 505-327-9811

Camping: Campgrounds are located 1 mile from the visitors center. Campers must provide their own wood or charcoal. Drinking water is available only at the visitors center.

Climate

Temperatures range in the 90s during the summer, with cold winter nights dropping below freezing. The area is located on a high semi-arid plateau of 6,301 feet. It experiences frequent thundershowers from July through September.

Features

The 8-mile-long, 2-mile-wide canyon is formed by steep sandstone cliffs. Chaco has 12 large ruins and more than 400 smaller ones.

About 1050 A.D., this area was one of the most important cultural centers in North America. Measuring 8 miles by 2 miles, it once had 16 towns, with population estimates between 5,000 and 7,000.

The large kiva (Fig. 27) at Casa Rinconada measures 63 feet across and held about 100 people. It is a good representation of the Chaco kiva complete with its sipapu, fire pit, underground ventilator shaft, floor vaults, roof supports, and circular benches around the exterior walls.

Pueblo Bonito, or "beautiful village," is 4 miles into the canyon, and covers over 3 acres. At one point it rose five stories, and contained over 750 rooms and numerous kivas, with a population of 1,200. The pueblo was probably the largest building of its kind in the southwest. The classic Pueblo-style building was built between 1030 and 1079, but the area was abandoned during the mid-1100s.

Activities

There is a long self-guided tour to Casa Rinconada, Chetro Ketl, the second largest pueblo,

Fig. 27. Kivas or ceremonial lodges were once the focal point of the community. (National Park Service Photo)

Pueblo del Arroyo and Pueblo Bonito. There are also conducted tours and special evening programs available at the visitors center.

Backcountry hikers can also enjoy hiking along four other outlying trails.

Information

Superintendent
Star Route #4
P.O. Box 6500
Bloomfield, NM 87413
505-786-5384

EL MORRO NATIONAL MONUMENT

The monument is 43 miles southwest of Grants and 56 miles southeast of Gallup.

Airports

Gallup Municipal, Albuquerque Sectional
Latitude: 35–30
Longitude: 108–47
FSS: 505-722-4308
Car rentals

Grants-Milan Municipal, Albuquerque Sectional
Latitude: 35–10
Longitude: 107–54
FSS: 800-432-6474
Taxi

Note: Grants is located on the northern edge of one of North America's largest lava beds. Some lava flows date back several million years to when Mt. Taylor, located 12 miles northeast of the city, erupted.

Season and Access

The monument has an all-weather access road open year-round. The best time to visit is from May to February.

Accommodations

In Gallup:
Ambassador Motel: 505-722-3843
Blue Spruce Inn: 505-863-9553
Rodeway Inn: 505-863-9383

In Grants:
Best Western: 505-287-7901
Grants TraveLodge: 505-287-2991
Holiday Inn: 505-287-4426
Stagecoach Inn: 505-287-2933

Camping: There is a small campground in the monument.

In Grants: Bluewater Lake State Park, Cibola Sands, and Coal Mine.

In Gallup: Gallup KOA and Red Rocks State Park

Features

El Morro, which means "headland" or bluff, is known for the famous "Inscription Rock", a 200-foot sandstone monolith. Ancestors of the Zuni Indians passing through the area left behind hundreds of inscriptions and petroglyphs on the smooth rock. Then, in the 1500s, Spaniards left records of their passage, followed by even later inscriptions by other Americans.

Two Indian villages once thrived on the mesa top. Part of the remains includes a 300- to 500-room building constructed in the thirteenth century.

In 1605, Don Juan de Onate, governor and colonizer of New Mexico, signed the rock. In 1629, Governor Manuel de Silva Nieto signed in, while the earliest English signature was that of Lt. Simpson in 1849.

Activities

Tour the visitors center.

Take the self-guided nature trail walk to the large rock outcrop, or follow the trail over the mesa top to visit the excavated Indian ruins.

Information

Superintendent
El Morro National Monument
Ramah, NM 87321
505-783-5132

GILA CLIFF DWELLINGS
NATIONAL MONUMENT

The ruins are located 45 miles north of Silver City near Lake Roberts.

Airport

Silver City-Grant County, Albuquerque Sectional
Latitude: 32–37
Longitude: 108–09
FSS: 505-388-1811
Car rental: 505-538-2142

Climate

The mid-summer weather is warm with frequent thunderstorms.

Accommodations

Copper Manor Motel, restaurant: 505-538-5392
Drifter Motel: 505-538-2916
Best Western Holiday Motor Hotel, restaurant:
    505-538-3711

Camping: Two campgrounds are located adjacent to the monument, Forks and Grapevine Campgrounds. Both are 5 miles from the visitors center. Neither has drinking water. Scorpion Campground is 1 mile from the visitors center.

At Gila Hot Springs, 4 miles from the monument, there are a campground, grocery store, and a vacation center: 505-534-9551.

Features

Visitors can see cliff dwelling rooms in Dweller Canyon that were constructed in the 1280s by peoples of the Mogollon culture. Natural archways lead from the largest shelter to other rooms. The walls were constructed of flat stones and adobe.

The inhabitants farmed and traded with other Indian tribes and were good weavers. Their pottery was brown and black and black on white. The area was abandoned in the 1400s.

Activities

To see the cliff dwellings, park in the monument parking lot and follow a ½-mile trail up Cliff Dweller Canyon.

Information

Contact at least three weeks in advance:
National Park Service Superintendent
P.O. Box 1320
Silver City, NM 88061

District Ranger
Wilderness Ranger District
Rt. 11, Box 100
Silver City, NM 88061

PECOS NATIONAL MONUMENT

The monument is located 26 miles southeast of Santa Fe.

Airport

Santa Fe County Municipal, Albuquerque Sectional
Latitude: 35–37
Longitude: 106–05
FSS: 505-982-3871
Car rentals

Accommodations

Best Western Inn, restaurant: 505-988-5531
Comfort Inn, restaurant: 505-471-8072
Garrett's Desert Inn, restaurant: 505-982-1851
Ramada Inn, restaurant: 505-471-3000

Camping in Pecos: Field Tract, Holy Ghost, and Iron Gate: 505-757-6121

Features

The Forked Lightning Ruin was inhabited in the 1200s, and was abandoned by 1300. Then the people moved to the Pecos pueblo, a multistoried building shaped in a rectangle. It was built to defend their reservoirs with a guardhouse at the entrance. There were also staggered entrance passageways and no exterior doors.

Two mission churches were established by the Spaniards, one dating to the seventeenth century and another 100 years later. The old Pecos mission was built over the ruins of a much larger church dating back to the 1620s.

The Indian population slowly decreased, and by 1838 the village had been abandoned and its inhabitants moved to Jemez Pueblo.

Activities

Take a 1-mile self-guided tour of the ruins. You may request guided tours.

Information

Superintendent
Drawer 11
Pecos, NM 87552
505-757-6414

SALINAS NATIONAL MONUMENT

The area is at 6,600 feet and 25 miles south of Mountainair.

Airport

Mountainair Municipal, Albuquerque Sectional
Latitude: 34–31
Longitude: 106–13
FSS: 505-243-7831

Accommodations

Trails End Motel: 505-847-2405

Camping: A campground is located 1 mile from the airport.

Features

The area was inhabited in 800 A.D. by Mogollon people, who farmed the dry land. At first they made crude brown pottery, but this soon changed to black on white pottery as the result of their contact with the pueblo people. They also adopted the kiva, an underground ceremonial chamber. By the 17th century, they occupied the largest pueblo village in the area, called the "pueblo de las Humanas" by the Spanish.

Spanish friars converted the people and built churches here, but didn't replace the kivas. Two of the Franciscan churches have been preserved: San Isidro, begun in 1628, and San Buenaventura, begun in 1660.

Activities

The visitors center is open daily.

There is a self-guiding walk along Mission Trail. You can see 21 Indian pueblos whose limestone rooms date back to 1300 A.D.

Information

Superintendent
Salinas National Monument
P.O. Box 496
Mountainair, NM 87036
505-847-2743

New York

CASTLE CLINTON NATIONAL MONUMENT

The castle is in New York City.

Airports

John F. Kennedy International, New York Sectional
Latitude: 40–38
Longitude: 73–47
FSS: 718-995-8657
Car rentals

Transportation: JFK Express trains operate daily every 20 minutes from 5:00 A.M. until midnight. Information: 718-858-7272. Also Carey Airport Express shuttles operate from here: 718-564-8484.

La Guardia, New York Sectional
Latitude: 40–46
Longitude: 73–52
FSS: 212-898-1550
Transportation: Shuttle bus, Carey Airport Express: 564-8484
Car rentals:
    Avis: 212-457-5500
    Hertz: 212-478-5300
    Budget: 212-478-7700

Newark International, New York Sectional
Latitude: 40–41
Longitude: 74–10
FSS: 212-288-3208
Rental cars: Avis, Hertz
Shuttle: Carey Airport Express

Accommodations

Near Broadway, theater district
    Hilton: 212-586-7000
    St. Regis-Sheraton: 212-753-4500
    Novotel: 212-315-0100

Features

Castle Clinton was built in 1807 in response to the British attack on the American frigate *Chesapeake*. At that time, five new forts were constructed including the Southwest Battery which was connected to Manhattan with a drawbridge. This fort was completed in 1811, and at the end of the War of 1812 became the headquarters for the Third Military District and renamed Castle Clinton after the former major and governor of New York.

In 1824, Clinton Castle became the entertainment center, with a garden used as a setting for many concerts. Castle Garden was used as a theater for over 25 years.

In 1835, Castle Garden became an immigration center, and between 1855 and 1889, over eight million immigrants passed through here. In 1896, it was used as the New York City Aquarium. In 1941, the aquarium closed.

Today the fortress is once again a concert site.

Information

Castle Clinton National Monument
26 Wall Street
New York City, NY 10005

FEDERAL HALL NATIONAL MEMORIAL

Federal Hall is in New York City, and faces City Hall Park. It's located at the corner of Wall Street and Nassau Street.

Features

Federal Hall is an outstanding example of Greek Revival architecture. Here you can see many historic objects and documents associated with the people and events of our nation's beginning. It was here that the Declaration of Independence was read to the Army on July 9, 1776, in the presence of General Washington.

The U.S. government began working here on March 4, 1789, since New York City was the first capital of the fledgling nation. Congress met here, with the Senate convening in one wing and the House in the other. George Washington was sworn into office here.

By 1790, the federal government had moved to Philadelphia and Federal Hall was no longer large enough to serve the governmental needs. In 1812, the old building was sold for salvage and the newer building, now referred to as the Customs Building, was completed in 1842.

The museum also has a display on Peter Zinger, whose trial served as one of the landmarks for freedom of the press. It's open Monday to Friday. For information, call 212-264-4367.

Pick up a schedule for the American Landmark Festivals listing of free events offered both at Federal Hall and at the TR Birthplace.

The monument itself is open by appointment only on Monday through Friday. Call 212-566-5700.

Information

Superintendent
Federal Hall National Memorial
26 Wall St.
New York City, NY 10005
212-264-8711

ROOSEVELT-VANDERBILT MANSION NATIONAL HISTORIC SITE,

FDR HOME NATIONAL HISTORIC SITE, AND ELEANOR ROOSEVELT NATIONAL HISTORIC SITE

The sites are in Hyde Park. The Vanderbilt Mansion is 2 miles north of the Roosevelt estate.

Airport

Dutchess City, New York Sectional
Latitude: 41–37
Longitude: 73–53
FSS: 212-462-3400

Accommodations

In Hyde Park:
    The Dutch Patroon Motel: 914-229-7141
    Roosevelt Inn: 914-229-0026
    Vanderbilt Motel: 914-229-7100
    Golden Manor Motel: 914-229-2157
    Bed and Breakfast: Mary Ann Martinez: 914-229-5937

Season

Roosevelt's home is open from 9:00 A.M. to 5:00 P.M., 7 days a week March through November, and from Thursday through Monday in December through February.

Features

The Roosevelt mansion is the site is the former home of FDR, the 32nd President. He lived here as a youth, and then later as a husband and father to five children.

The home dates back to the early 1800s. It was sometimes called Roosevelt's "Summer White House." Here in 1942, Roosevelt and Winston Churchill signed an agreement leading to the use of the first atomic bomb. It was also the site of his last campaign speech prior to his becoming President for the fourth time.

Val-Kill Cottage was used as a gathering place for many of the world's notables, who came to see FDR's grave and to pay their respects to his widow.

The Vanderbilt mansion, (Fig. 28) home of Frederick Vanderbilt, is one of the finest examples of Italian Renaissance architecture in the United States. The Pavilion was constructed in 1895, and later the 54 room mansion was completed.

Activities

Purchase a combination ticket for admittance to the FDR Library, museum, FDR Home, and Vanderbilt Mansion.

While here, also visit the Eleanor Roosevelt National Historic Site. A shuttle bus takes you there from April to October, 7 days a week. From November to March, it's open Thursday to Monday. The site is closed from December to February except by reservation.

You can also tour the James Vanderpoll House of History and the Van Alen House with a combination ticket. For information, call 914-758-9265.

Information

Superintendent
Roosevelt-Vanderbilt National Historic Site
Hyde Park, NY 12538
914-229-9115

SARATOGA NATIONAL HISTORICAL PARK

The park is north of New York City, in the foothills

Fig. 28. Vanderbilt Mansion National Historic Site, home of Frederick Vanderbilt.

of the Adirondack Mountains, and southeast of Saratoga Springs.

Airport

Saratoga County, New York Sectional
Latitude: 43–03
Longitude: 73–52
FSS: 914-869-9225 or 800-342-4524

Accommodations

Best Western-Playmore Farms: 518-584-2350
Holiday Inn, restaurant: 518-584-4550
The Springs Motel: 518-584-6336

Features

On September 19 and October 7, 1777, General Horatio Gates, commanding the American Army, defeated the British Redcoats led by "Gentleman Johnny" Burgoyne during the Revolutionary War. The victory was decisive in preventing the British from controlling the Hudson, and is one of the 15 most decisive battles in world history. Following the American victory, the war was moved to the south and to the sea. It also resulted in the French joining the Americans as allies, which eventually led to victory at Yorktown.

Activities

Tour the visitors center and watch a 21-minute film, *Checkmate on the Hudson.*

Drive the 9-mile Tour Road, passing the points of historic interest. It's open from April 15 to November 30, weather permitting. Runners and hikers will find markers along the tour road every ¼ mile. Bicyclists should park in the lower lot and be ready for a steep winding downgrade beginning at Stop 10, followed by a 1½-mile uphill climb back to the visitors center parking lot.

Tour the restored General Philip Schuyler House open from late June to Labor Day, and the Saratoga Monument, both located 8 miles from the battlefield. Also hike a steep 1-mile loop past the grave of Gen. Simon Fraser.

Visit nearby Saratoga Springs, once the most celebrated spa in the United States. Attend concerts during the summer in the Saratoga Spa State Park's Performing Arts Center, summer home for the New York City Ballet and Philadelphia Symphony Orchestra. Ticket information: 518-584-2000 or 518-587-3330.

Treat yourself to a bath and massage at the Saratoga Spa.

Tour the National Museum of Racing and Thoroughbred Hall of Fame on Union Avenue.

Information

Saratoga National Historical Park
RD #2, Box 33
Stillwater, NY 12170
518-664-9821

STATUE OF LIBERTY NATIONAL MEMORIAL

This famous statue is located in Upper New York Bay on Liberty Island. It was the first stopping point for many early twentieth century immigrants, and today can be reached by boat from the Battery.

Features

The monument was designed to commemorate the alliance of France and the United States during the War for Independence in 1884. The two nations' friendship began when the French assisted the struggling colonies in their battle for independence from England.

The statue was French historian Edouard de Laboulage's original idea, and he engaged an Alsatian sculptor, Frederic Bartholdi, to sculpt it. The statue was built in France and disassembled into over 200 cases to be shipped to America. It stands 151 feet high, and with its pedestal of 156 feet, it's the tallest statue known in modern times.

The poem that appears on a bronze plaque on the base of the monument was written by Emma Lazarus in 1883, and was entitled "The New Colossus." It reads "Give me your tired, your poor, your huddled masses yearning to breathe free. The wretched refuse of your teeming shore. Send these, the homeless, tempest-tost to me. I lift my lamp beside the golden door.''

Ellis Island was begun as a landfill project, serving first as an arsenal and fort. In 1892, it became an immigration center. Between 1905 and 1914, an average of one million people arrived on the island's center each year.

Activities

We were able to get a fantastic view of this statue by contacting the flight authorities for permission for a fly-by.

Take a ferry to the statue via Circle Line Ferries located in Battery Park in lower Manhattan. They depart every hour. For information, call 212-269-5755.

The American Museum of Immigration is located in the statue's base, where you can see the history of U.S. immigration. It's open Monday to Friday 9:00 A.M. to 5:00 P.M. For information, call 212-264-8711.

Visitors can take an elevator to the balcony near the top of the stonework. A spiral staircase leads to an observation platform located within the statue's head.

The Statue of Liberty officially celebrated her 100th birthday on October 28, 1986. To celebrate, the statue was fully restored with new stainless steel interior supports, a new torch, a glass-walled hydraulic elevator, a new dock area, and service buildings that will accommodate two million annual visitors.

THEODORE ROOSEVELT BIRTHPLACE NATIONAL HISTORIC SITE

The home is at 28 East 20th Street, located between Fifth Avenue and Park Avenue in New York City.

Features

The five-story brownstone is a reconstruction of the original home, which was torn down in 1916. It contains approximately 40 percent of the original furnishings. Continuous tours are offered Wednes-

day through Sunday, 9:00 A.M. to 5:00 P.M. It has a great museum, and includes the shirt Roosevelt was wearing when an assassination attempt was made on his life.

Information

Superintendent
26 Wall St.
New York, NY 10005
212-260-1616

Additional Attractions in New York City

The *Intrepid* Sea-Air-Space Museum is located in Pier 86. See an aircraft carrier converted into a museum. For information, call 245-0072.

Fire Island National Seashore offers hiking, surf fishing, and touring of Sunken Forest west of Sailors Haven. Access to the seashore is from the east and west ends of the park. Ferries operate from the mainland May to November. Access is from Sailors Haven, Watch Hill, Smith Point, and Patchogue.

Brooklyn Bridge: Park Row and City Hall. This historic bridge overlooking the East River links Manhattan and Brooklyn, and includes a walkway for pedestrians as well as a bikepath.

Central Park, located between Fifth Avenue and Central Park West from 59th Street to 110th Street, is a must for bikers and runners. It also has a children's zoo and a skating rink. Also, take a horse and carriage ride through the park. Rides begin on the 59th Street side of the park.

Bicyclists can also enjoy riding in Prospect Park, or along either Shore Road or Shore Parkway in Brooklyn.

Runners interested in participating in a weekend race sponsored by the New York Road Runners should either go by their headquarters near Central Park at 9 East 89th, or call 860-4455.

The Empire State Building between 33rd and 34th Street on Fifth Avenue stands 1,472 feet high, and was once the tallest building in the world. Get a view of the city from the 86th and 102nd floors. It's open daily 9:30 A.M. until midnight.

Lincoln Center for the Performing Arts, located at Broadway at 65th Street, offers many cultural events performances by the New York Philharmonic, New York City Opera, and the New York City Ballet Company. Take a guided tour daily from 10:30 A.M. to 5:00 P.M. Information: 212-877-1800, extension 512.

St. Patrick's Cathedral at Fifth Avenue and 50th Street is a beautiful Roman Catholic Church with towers that rise over 330 feet.

The South Street Seaport located at Fulton Street and South Street features a museum five blocks long with historic shops, four historic ships, and an old printing shop. Take a tour and see shows presented hourly beginning at 11:00 A.M. Summer concerts. Information: 669-9400. General information: 212-608-7888.

The World Trade Center on Liberty Street has the second tallest skyscrapers in the world, each 110 stories high. It has the highest open-air observation deck with a great view of New York and New Jersey. It's open daily from 9:30 A.M. to 9:30 P.M. Information: 212-466-7377. During good weather, lunchtime concerts are offered from 12:15 to 1:30 P.M. For information, call 212-466-4170.

See "The New York Experience," a multimedia presentation, from 11:00 A.M. to 7:00 P.M. at the McGraw-Hill Building at 1221 Avenue of the Americas. For information, call 869-0345.

Radio City Music Hall offers tours, "Backstage at Radio City Music Hall." See the famous Rockettes in performance. For information, call 212-541-9436. For a show schedule and information 212-757-3100.

Take a Sunday Walking Tour sponsored by the Musicians of the City of New York. For information, call 212-534-1672.

Attend a concert at Carnegie Hall. Tickets may be ordered by phone. Call 247-7800.

Take a 3-hour cruise around Manhattan Island. Call 212-563-3200.

Visit the New York Stock Exchange. Automated narration Mondays through Fridays from 10:00 A.M. to 4:00 P.M. Admission is free. For information, call 212-623-5168.

To obtain tickets at a 50 percent discount on the day of the performance to shows both on and off Broadway and at Lincoln Center, visit the TKTS office in Bryant Park on 42nd Street; at the Times Square Theater Center, 47th and Broadway; or on the mezzanine at 2 World Trade Center.

For Discount "Twofers," go to New York Convention and Visitors Center, 2 Columbus Circle, or call 212-397-8222.

Visit UN Headquarters and see 158 flags representing the member states. It has three main buildings. Free tickets are available in the Visitors Lobby for the General Assembly, which meets from September to December. Hour-long tours are offered every 15 minutes from 9:15 A.M. to 4:45 P.M. Information: 212-754-4440 or 212-754-7713.

Walk through Tiffany's at Fifth Avenue and 57th and see a wonderful jewelry, sterling silver, china, and crystal selection.

Follow the Heritage Trail, a 3-mile-long self-guided tour with 17 markers. Begin at Civic Center downtown. You go past Trinity Church, the New York Stock Exchange, and Battery Park, where you can catch a ferry to Staten Island for $.25. Maps are available at Federal Hall.

Tour the Federal Reserve Bank of New York. One-hour tours Monday through Friday at 10:00 A.M., 11:00 A.M., 1:00 P.M., and 2:00 P.M.. Reservations must be requested at least a week in advance, but they're free. Call 212-791-6130.

Tour Lincoln Center seven days a week from 10:00 A.M. to 5:00 P.M. For information, call 212-877-1800. Attend a concert in one of its three auditoriums.

Take a tour of the NBC Studios at 30 Rockefeller Plaza. For information, call 212-664-4000.

New York City is well known for its many museums, including the Metropolitan Museum of Art at 82nd and Fifth Avenue, and the Museum of Natural History at W. 77th near Central Park.

To reach West Point without having to drive there, take a day-long cruise on the Hudson River Day Line. Information: 212-279-5151.

Information

New York events: 212-755-4100
Bus and subway: 718-330-1234

WEST POINT

West Point is southeast of Newburgh along the Hudson River.

Airport

Ramapo Valley, New York Sectional
Latitude: 41–06
Longitude: 74–01
FSS: 800-526-4704

Accommodations

In Highland Falls:
Hotel Thayer, restaurant: 914-446-4781
West Point Motel: 914-446-4180
Palisades Motel: 914-446-9400
U.S. Academy Motel: 914-446-2021

Features

West Point was the base for Baron Von Steuben's American Revolutionary War forces, who marched along the grounds over 200 years ago. In 1802, the ''Point'' became home to the U.S. Army academy, making it the nation's oldest military academy.

Revolutionary War fortifications and battlegrounds tell the story of our early struggles. Today approximately 4,000 cadets live here as they prepare for careers as Army officers.

You can take a 1-hour guided bus tour of the grounds at 11:00 A.M. and 1:00 P.M. Monday through Friday, or Saturday and Sunday from 10:00 A.M. to 2:30 P.M. or pick up brochures and maps at the Visitors Information Center outside the main gate at Highland Falls and do it on your own.

Tour the West Point Museum to see the largest collection of military arms in the Western Hemisphere. The museum is free and is open from 10:30 A.M. to 4:15 P.M. daily.

Check with the Eisenhower Theater to see if any band, chamber concerts, or Broadway productions are being presented. During the summer, the academy band offers outdoor concerts in the amphitheater at Trophy Point.

Cadet parades are held in the spring and fall. For information: 914-938-2638.

Cadet Chapel has fantastic stained glass windows and one of the biggest church organs in the world. It's open daily from 8 to 4:15 (Fig. 29).

From the museum, walk over to Trophy Point to get the famous view painters have portrayed of the Hudson River and site of the Battle Monument which is engraved with the names of 2,240 Union Army soldiers killed in the Civil War. You can also see some links from the big chain that had been stretched across the river to prevent the British from controlling the Hudson and splitting the colonies.

Tour Fort Putnam, a restored Revolutionary War fort, located above the stadium.

If you reach here early enough, you can take a boat tour of the Highlands that leaves from the West Point south dock at 12:30 P.M. daily.

Additional Attractions

Other homes along the Hudson include Olana, a state historic site. It's a nineteenth-century Persian-style castle. Information: 518-828-0135.

You can also see ''Sunnyside,'' Washington Irving's ''Cottage;'' Clermont, home of Robert Livingston, one of the drafters of the Declaration of Independence; and the home of President Martin Van Buren, our eighth President. Tours are offered Wednesday through Sunday from Memorial Day through Labor Day. Information: 518-758-9689.

The old Rhinebeck Aerodome, approximately 15 miles north of the Vanderbilt Mansion, has vintage airplanes and weekend airshows at 2:30 P.M.. Take a biplane ride. It's open May 15 to October 15 from 10:00 A.M. to 5:00 P.M.

Information

Hudson River Valley Association
72 Main St.
Cold Spring-on-Hudson, NY 10516
914-265-3066

Fig. 29. Cadet Chapel, West Point, contains one of the largest church organs in the world.

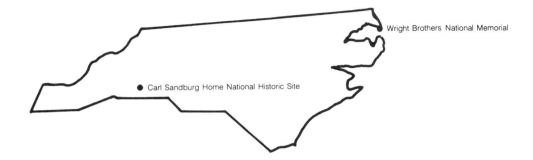

Carl Sandburg Home National Historic Site

Wright Brothers National Memorial

North Carolina

CARL SANDBURG
NATIONAL HISTORIC SITE

The Sandburg home is in Flat Rock, 4 miles south of Hendersonville, or 26 miles south of Asheville. Turn off US 25 onto Little River Road at the Flat Rock Playhouse to reach the park.

Airports

Hendersonville, Atlanta Sectional
Latitude: 35–18
Longitude: 82–26
FSS: 800-922-1816
No car rentals are available.
　　The airport is 5 miles from the home.

Asheville Regional, Atlanta Sectional
Latitude: 35–26
Longitude: 82–32
FSS: 704-684-2301
WS: 704-684-3787
Car rentals:
　　Budget: 704-684-2272
　　Hertz: 704-684-6455
　　National: 704-684-8572

Accommodations

In Hendersonville:
　　Cabins in the Pines: 704-692-3110
　　Pine Acres Motel: 704-693-0496
　　Old Mill Motel: 704-693-6077
　　Bed and Breakfast: The Waverly: 704-693-9193

　　Camping in Holmes State Forest. Walk-in tent sites are available March 15 to November 30.

In Asheville:
　　Best Western: 704-298-5562
　　Forest Manor Motor Lodge: 704-274-3531
　　Econo Lodge: 704-298-5519

Features

　　"Connemara" was Carl Sandburg's home during his last 22 years. Here, he published his only novel and completed his autobiography, plus several volumes of history and poetry.

Activities

　　Tour the home and follow self-guided walks about the grounds.

Nearby Attractions

In Asheville, tour the Biltmore House and Gardens, a 255-room mansion resembling a French Renaissance home. The mansion is surrounded by an estate of 8,000 acres. For information, call 704-274- 1776.

Visit nearby Chimney Rock, a 215-foot granite monolith. Access to its summit is via trail, stairs, or elevator. Follow trails to several scenic areas including Hickory Nut Falls, with a waterfall double to that found at Niagara Falls. For information, call 704-625-9611.

Tour Craggy Gardens, 17 miles from town, especially in mid-June when the rhododendron are blooming. Hiking is available.

Information

Superintendent
Carl Sandburg Home National Historic Site
P.O. Box 395
Flat Rock, NC 28731
704-693-4178

WRIGHT BROTHERS NATIONAL MEMORIAL

The memorial is between Kitty Hawk and Nags Head on North Carolina's Outer Banks.

Airport

First Flight, Charlotte Sectional
Latitude: 36–01
Longitude: 75–40
Parking on the airstrip is limited to 24 consecutive hours. No gas is available.

Manteo-Dare County Regional, Charlotte Sectional
Latitude: 35–55
Longitude: 75–41
FSS: 800-682-2649
Car rentals

James M. Cox Dayton International
    Cincinnati Sectional
Latitude: 39–54

Longitude: 84–13
FSS: 898-3692
Car rentals
The airport is 15 miles from the memorial.

Accommodations

In Hatteras:
    Hatteras Harbor Motel: 704-986-2565
    Hatteras Inn Cabanas: 704-986-2241
    Hatteras Island Inn: 704-987-2345
    Hatteras Marlin Motel: 704-986-2141

In Kitty Hawk:
    Buccaneer: 919-261-2030
    The Beach House: 919-261-2921
    Anderson's Beach Cottages: 919-261-2727

In Manteo:
    Duke of Dare Motor Lodge: 919-473-2175

Camping: A campground is located at Cape Hatteras.

Climate

It's generally windy with moderate temperatures. However, hurricane season extends from June to November, with the most frequent ones coming in August and September.

Features

The Wright Brothers were truly geniuses. After they discovered they had based their original theories on flying on incorrect aeronautical data compiled by others, they conducted extensive experiments on their own. They eventually designed and flew their glider over 1,000 flights.

They designed their own four-cylinder engine, since none was available. Then these two men, who had only completed high school and had no advanced education in engineering, designed and built their own propeller, which proved to be very successful the first time it was ever tested. They also built one of the world's first wind tunnels in order to test their airfoil design.

The "Flyer" they designed had a 40-foot wing-span, a 12-horsepower engine and weighed 170 pounds. On December 17, 1903, it was launched, flying 120 feet and staying in the air 12 seconds. The fourth and final flight made that day soared over 850 feet.

Activities

The visitors center has a full-scale reproduction of the original plane, exhibits, and lectures on the Wright Brothers. Visit the Wright's 1902-3 camp buildings.

You can easily walk to the Wright Monument Shaft from the strip. It's located on top of Kill Devil Hill, a 90-foot dune of once-shifting sands, site of many of their glider experiments.

While in the area you can rent some high-performance catamarans, go windsurfing along the protected waters of the sound, or go hang gliding on the sand dunes of Jockey's Ridge State Park, south of Nags Head.

Nearby Attractions

Fort Raleigh National Historic Site is located on the northern tip of Roanoke Island, and 3 miles north of Manteo. Four hundred years ago it was the site of the struggle for 250 colonists, sent out by Sir Walter Raleigh. You can see the reconstruction of the small earthen fort and small settlement they built.

Attend a dramatic presentation at the Waterside Theater at 8:30 P.M. of "The Lost Colony," presented nightly except Sunday from mid-June to September 1st, and learn the story of the ill-fated people.

Cycle 70 miles along the Cape Hatteras National Seashore. This is best done other than during tourist season. Or cycle to Coquina Beach and search for the Laura Barnes, a ship wrecked in 1921. It's sometimes covered by the sand. Naturalists offer guided beach walks.

Information

Superintendent
Wright Brothers
c/o Cape Hatteras National Seashore
Rt 1, Box 675
Manteo, NC 27965
919-441-7430

● Theodore Roosevelt National Park

North Dakota

THEODORE ROOSEVELT NATIONAL PARK

The park has two units, a North Unit near Watford City and a South Unit near Medora. It's in the Badlands of North Dakota.

Airports

Watford City Municipal, Billings Sectional
Latitude: 47–47–58
Longitude: 103–15
FSS: 701-852-3696
Courtesy car

Williston-Sloulin Field International, Billings Sectional
Latitude: 48–10
Longitude: 103–3
FSS: 701-572-4414
Car rentals

Beach, Billings Sectional
Latitude: 46–55
Longitude: 103–58
FSS: 701-225-2989
Car rentals

There is a small, unimproved dirt landing strip near Medora, which the U.S. Forest Service plans to close in the near future.

Climate and Season

Mild, warm, and often hot days; cool nights. Weather can change suddenly, so be prepared for occasional violent storms. Rain falls mostly from May through July and averages 15 inches annually.

Even though the park is open all year, it's best to visit sometime from May through October. Parts of the park road close during the winter. Most Medora attractions are closed from Labor Day to Memorial Day.

Accommodations

In Medora:
Bad Lands Motel: 701-623-4422 or
701-223-4800 (off season)
Dietz's Motel: 701-623-4455
Medora Motel: 701-623-4422 or 701-223-4800
(off season)
Rough Riders Hotel: 623-4422

In Watford City:
Super 8 Lodge Motel: 701-842-3686
Four Eyes Motel: 701-842-2306
Park Hotel: 701-842-3575

In Beach:
Buckboard Inn: 701-872-4794
The Outpost: 701-872-4717
Westgate Motel: 701-872-4521

In Williston:
Econ-O-Inn: 701-572-4242
Super 8 Motel: 701-572-8371
Best Western: 701-572-6321

Camping: Cottonwood Campground in the park, entrance at Medora, or at Squaw Creek Campground in the park's North Unit.

Features

This land was one of Roosevelt's favorite spots. He came here as a rancher in 1883.

From Painted Canyon Overlook in the south part, you can see quite a view of the buttes, bluffs, and sharply eroded valleys. At one time, broad rivers deposited thick layers of sediment on a broad plain. In places, iron-rich minerals have stained the rocks yellow and buff.

At Scoria Point, the massive bluffs have been capped with red scoria, including a vein of lignite that burned and baked the sand and clay into the natural brick we see today. These thick black layers of lignite formed seams of low-grade coal.

Historic Medora is a restored pioneer cattle town from the late 1800s.

Activities

Medora is located in the south unit. Tour the De Mores Historic Site and see a 26-room chateau with many of the original furnishings owned by the Marquis de Mores. Tours are conducted daily from May through October 31. The rest of the year they're done by appointment only: Call 701-623-4355.

Tour the visitors center inside the Medora entrance. See Roosevelt's first cabin from the Maltese Cross Ranch. It's open year-round.

Attend the Medora Musical in an open-air theater and see some acts performed in Teddy Roosevelt's honor. For information, call 701-623-4444.

The area has several hiking trails in the North Unit, including Caprock Coulee Nature Trail (1½ miles), Caprook Coulee Trail (4-mile loop), Sperati Point and Achenbach Trail (11 miles).

In the South Unit, you can hike the Coal Vein Trail, Jones Creek Trail (3⁷⁄₁₀ miles) or Petrified Forest Trail. Don't drink the backcountry water.

Take the 13-mile scenic drive from the entrance station to Oxbow Overlook.

Information

Theodore Roosevelt National Park
Medora, ND 58645
701-623-4466

James A. Garfield National Historic Site

Neil Armstrong Air And Space Museum

Mound City Group National Monument

William Taft National Historic Site

Ohio

MOUND CITY GROUP NATIONAL MONUMENT

The monument is located 3 miles north of Chillicothe, Ohio.

Airport

Chillicothe-Ross County, Cincinnati Sectional
Latitude: 39–26
Longitude: 83–01
FSS: 513-871-6200
Car rentals

Accommodations

In Chillicothe:
    Holiday Inn: 513-775-7000
    L-K Motel: 513-775-2500
    Chillicothe Bed and Breakfast: 513-772-6848

Features

The "Hopewell" people located in the valley of the Scioto in southern Ohio, and lived here for at least 1,000 years. The culture apparently ended around 500 A.D.

The Indians had a system of rank distinctions in which people maintained a definite social order. It's believed that these mounds were built as memorials for their high-ranking dead. Borrow pits from which the necessary dirt was obtained are still visible within the monument.

Archeologists excavated the area in 1846 and found interesting artifacts, including stone tobacco pipes carved in the shapes of human heads, birds, and animals. They must have done trading with others, as their artifacts utilized obsidian (possibly from Yellowstone), mica from North Carolina, copper (possibly from Lake Superior), shells from the Gulf of Mexico, and the teeth of grizzly bears. Unfortunately, these artifacts are not available for public viewing, since they were sent to the British Museum.

Activities

Take a self-guided tour of the necropolis. Be alert for poison ivy. See the Mica Grave mound, which contained four bodies, all cremated. Many artifacts were recovered from here.

Another mound had some fossil mammoth and mastadon bones, along with pottery, copper, and shell ornaments.

125

Charnell House is where they cremated their dead.

At 9:00 P.M. each summer Saturday attend a special slide program.

Information

Superintendent
Mound City Group National Monument
16062 State Route 104
Chillicothe, OH 45601
614-744-1125

WILLIAM TAFT NATIONAL HISTORICAL SITE

William Taft National Historic Site is at 2038 Auburn Avenue, Cincinnati. The site preserves the birthplace and home of the only man to serve as both President and Chief Justice of the United States. It's open year-round.

Airport

Cincinnati Municipal
Latitude: 39–06
Longitude: 84–26
FSS: 513-871-8220

NEIL ARMSTRONG AIR AND SPACE MUSEUM

Northwest of the Mound City Group is Wapakoneta, site of the Neil Armstrong Air and Space Museum. See the history of flight depicted beginning with balloons and moving to space travel. Gemini 8 is also on display. For information, call 419-738-8811.

Airport

Wapakoneta-Neil Armstrong
Detroit Sectional
Latitude: 40–29

Longitude: 84–18
FSS: 513-898-3692

If you are in the northern part of the state, overfly Perry's Victory and International Peace Memorial on South Bass Island. To tour it from the ground, take a ferry to the memorial from Catawba Point and Port Clinton. For information, call 419-285-2184.

Airports

Carl R. Keller, Detroit Sectional
Latitude: 41–31
Longitude: 82–53
FSS: 216-535-6153

Put-In-Bay, Detroit Sectional
Latitude: 41–38
Longitude: 82–49
FSS: 216-625-6050

JAMES A. GARFIELD NATIONAL HISTORIC SITE

Also in the northern part of the state near Cleveland, see the James A. Garfield National Historic Site in Mentor, Ohio. His house is open year-round Tuesday through Saturday 10:00 A.M. to 5:00 P.M., Sunday from Noon to 5:00 P.M., and closed Monday. For information, call 216-255-8755.

Enjoy Cuyahoga Valley NRA, located southeast of Cleveland. The area encompasses 20 miles along the Cuyahoga River and runs along the old Ohio and Erie Canal.

Airport

Cuyahoga County, Detroit Sectional
Latitude: 41–34
Longitude: 81–29
FSS: 216-267-3700
Car rentals: Hertz: 216-261-5900

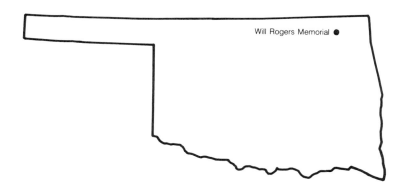

Will Rogers Memorial ●

Oklahoma

WILL ROGERS MEMORIAL

The Will Rogers Memorial is 1 mile west of Claremont.

Airports

Sam Riggs Airpark, Kansas City Sectional
Latitude: 36–13
Longitude: 97–38
FSS: 800-722-4988
Car rentals

Tulsa International, Kansas City Sectional
Latitude: 36–11
Longitude: 95–53
FSS: 800-722-4988
Car rentals
The airport is 25 miles from the park.

Accommodations

In Claremore:
Will Rogers Hotel: 918-341-0861
Best Western Will Rogers Motor Inn, restaurant: 918-341-4410

Motel Claremore: 918-341-3254

In Tulsa:
Best Western Trade Winds Central Inn, restaurant: 918-749-5561
Econo Lodge, restaurant: 918-438-5050
Quality Inn-Airport, restaurant: 918-438-0780

Features

The site includes four galleries containing much memorabilia of Will Rogers' life.

Activities

Rogers' birthplace, Oologah, is 12 miles northwest of town. Watch a 20-minute video on his life, plus another movie shown daily at 2.

Also tour the J.M. Davis Gun Museum to see one of the largest gun collections in the world, plus 75 antique instruments and over 600 World War I posters. For information, call 918-341-5707.

Information

918-341-0719

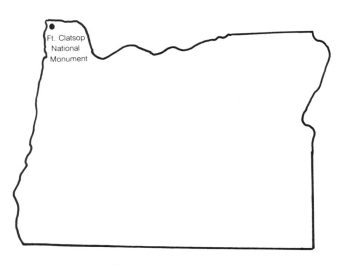

Oregon

FT. CLATSOP NATIONAL MONUMENT

The monument is 6 miles southwest of Astoria.

Airport

Port of Astoria, Seattle Sectional
Latitude: 46–09
Longitude: 123–53
FSS: 503-648-1022 or 800-462-8855
Rental cars:
    Hovell Auto: 503-325-2211
    Sunset Ford: 503-325-6411
    Hertz: 503-325-7700

Accommodations

The Astoria Dunes, restaurant: 503-325-7111
Bay View Motel: 503-325-1211
Thunderbird Motor Inn, restaurant:
    503- 325-7373

Climate

Temperatures January to March average 45° F; April to June, 53° F; July to September, 59° F; and October to December, 50° F.

Features

The memorial has a replica of the log fort built in 1805 by Lewis and Clark, who wintered here during 1805–06. Their expedition provided the first detailed knowledge of the northwest and helped bring trappers and settlers into the region.

Lewis and Clark spent 2½ years exploring previously unknown lands between Yellowstone and the lower cascades of the Columbia, expanding American scientific and geographic knowledge of the area.

Activities

Watch the living history program displaying the clothing, equipment, and lifestyle of those accompanying the explorers on their expedition. It's presented daily 9:30 A.M. to 5:30 P.M. from mid-June to Labor Day.

To see the salt cairn used by the expedition members, drive down to Seaside's southern end of the Promenade on Lewis and Clark Way. There you'll find a replica of the cairn built to extract salt from sea water, enabling the explorers to cure elk and deer for their return to St. Louis in 1806.

During the spring, you'll find good clam digging during low daytime tides. During the summer, the salmon fishing is excellent. Fall features great nighttime clamming.

Bicyclists can begin cycling on the Oregon Coast Bike Route, which follows the coastline. Maps are available at the park service headquarters.

Visit Ft. Stevens State Park in Hammond to see a reconstructed Civil War fort, which remained active through World War II. You'll see concrete gun batteries and a museum.

Hikers have access to the beginning of the 64-mile Oregon Coast Trail, which begins at Ft. Stevens and goes south to Barview near Garibaldi.

Also watch for the rusting hulk of the *Peter Iredale*, a 4-masted British ship.

Fort Astoria, erected in 1811, was the first permanent American outpost west of the Mississippi. You'll see a recreation of the fort at Exchange and 15th Streets.

Tour the Columbia River Maritime Museum.

Warrentown and Hammond, a few miles south of Astoria, are sport fishing centers. Fishermen can contact Thunderbird Charters at 503-325-7990.

Information

Superintendent
Ft. Clatsop National Monument
Rt. 3, Box 604 F-C
Astoria, OR 97013
503-861-2471

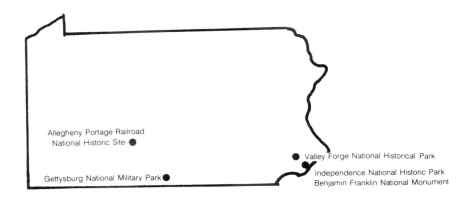

Allegheny Portage Railroad National Historic Site

Valley Forge National Historical Park

Independence National Historic Park
Benjamin Franklin National Monument

Gettysburg National Military Park

Pennsylvania

ALLEGHENY PORTAGE RAILROAD NATIONAL HISTORIC SITE

The site is two miles east of Cresson, Pennsylvania.

Airport

Altoona-Blair County, Detroit Sectional
Latitude: 40–17
Longitude: 78–19
FSS: 800-252-3887 or 814-793-3113

Accommodations

In Altoona:
    Sheraton: 814-946-4581
    Holiday Inn: 814-944-4581
    Minuet Manor Motel: 814-742-8441

Features

The portage railroad was constructed to carry canal boats 1,400 feet over the mountains between Hollidaysburg and Johnstown. The boats were placed on flatbed cars and hauled over the mountains via the inclined plane railroad. With its construction, the railroad and the canal provided continuous transportation between Pittsburgh and Philadelphia and served as a major route for the settlers going west. However, it was abandoned in 1857 when railroads crossed the mountains.

Activities

Stop by the Lemon House, built near the summit of Allegheny Mountain. Once a tavern, it is now the visitors center. Watch the 12-minute slide program.

Hike along interpretative trails including Stone Quarry Trail, Incline 6 Trail, Summit Level, and Summit Nature trails.

Information

Superintendent
Allegheny Portage Railroad National Historic Site
P.O. Box 247
Cresson, PA 16630
814-886-8176

Nearby Attractions

For fishing and boating, visit Prince Gallitzin State Park, or tour the Schwab Gardens in Loretto, once owned by millionaire Charles Schwab.

The Johnstown National Memorial is a reminder of the nation's deadliest flood. When the earthen dam gave way, over 2,200 people lost their lives. Visit the Johnstown Flood Museum in town to see a slide show depicting the three devastating floods that tore through town. Closed Mondays. The memorial itself is north of town and is open daily. For information, call 814-886-8176.

BENJAMIN FRANKLIN NATIONAL MEMORIAL AND INDEPENDENCE NATIONAL HISTORICAL PARK

The park and memorial are in Philadelphia.

Airports

Northeast Philadelphia, New York Sectional
Latitude: 40–05
Longitude: 75–00
FSS: 215-673-8020
Car rentals:
    Avis: 215-492-0900
    Budget: 215-492-3915
    Hertz: 215-492-2902

Philadelphia-Wings, New York Sectional
Latitude: 40–08
Longitude: 75–16
FSS: 215-673-8020 or 800-822-3750
Car rentals: Budget: 800-527-0700

Philadelphia International, New York Sectional
Latitude: 39–52
Longitude: 75–14
FSS: 215-673-8020
Car Rentals:
    Hertz: 215-492-7200
    Avis: 215-492-0900
    National: 215-492-2750

Climate

The warmest month is July; January is the col-
dest and rainiest with 4½ inches of precipitation. Spring and fall bring moderate temperatures.

Accommodations

Holiday Inn-Independence Mall: 215-923-8660
Airport Ramada Inn: 215-521-9600
Best Western Monticello Motor Lodge: 609-931-0700
Bed and Breakfast in private homes: 215-735-1137 or 215-884-1084

Features

Philadelphia has America's most historic square mile, including Independence Hall and the Liberty Bell, plus the Benjamin Franklin National Monument (Fig. 30).

The Declaration of Independence was written here in 1776 by the Second Continental Congress. In 1787, the city served as the site of the Constitutional Convention. It served as the Revolutionary War capital during the British occupation, and as the nation's capital until 1800.

Activities

Visit the visitors center at Third and Chestnut and obtain a free tour ticket for the Todd House, home of Dolly Madison. Watch the 28-minute film *Independence*.

Visit City Tavern and enjoy lunch or dinner, and Carpenter's Hall, site of the First Continental Congress. Carpenter's Hall is open Tuesday through Sunday from 10:00 A.M. to 4:00 P.M..

A short distance from Independence Hall is Franklin Court, site of Ben Franklin's home. Tour the underground museum featuring a multi-media presentation on Franklin and watch a 20-minute movie on his life.

Tour Independence Hall. Get there early during the summer. Stop by the Liberty Bell Pavilion, where brief ranger talks are given.

Near Independence Park is Old City, with more historic sites. Elfreth's Alley, the oldest continuously occupied residential American street, is between Front and Second. You'll see 30 houses built

Fig. 30. Independence Hall, Independence National Historical Park. (National Park Service Photo by Richard Frear)

between 1713 and 1811. A museum is located in #126, open 7 days a week from March to December 15 from 10:00 A.M. to 4:00 P.M. For information, call 215-574-0560. Betsy Ross' house is nearby and open for tours.

The U.S.S. *Olympia* is docked at Penn's Landing. The ship dates back to the Spanish-American War. You can also see a World War II sub and one of the last steel "tall ships" afloat.

Fairmont Park is the largest landscaped city park in the world, where there are 75 miles of hiking trails and 25 miles for cycling. You can rent both sailboats and bicycles here: 215-236-4359 or 215-978-8545. Runners generally run along Benjamin Franklin Parkway or along East River Drive in Fairmont Park.

You can also take an historic house tour. The houses are closed Mondays, and are accessible via the Fairmont Park Trolley Bus Tour. For information, call 215-787-5449.

Franklin Institute is a "hands-on" science and technological museum. See the world's largest walkthrough heart. Open 7 days a week. Call 215-564-3375.

Visit Longwood Gardens on Kennett Square. Watch Festival of Fountains, featuring ½-hour presentations of the illuminated fountains Tuesday, Thursday, and Saturday evenings beginning at 9:15 from June to August. For information, call 215-388-6741.

The Norman Rockwell Museum has a collection of all the famous painter's *Saturday Evening Post* covers. For information, call 215-922-4345.

The Brandywine River Museum at Chadds Ford is a preserved century-old grist mill now used as a museum with a collection of American art.

Ride aboard a mule-drawn barge led along the Delaware Canal in New Hope. For information, call 215-862-2842.

The Pearl S. Buck Estate is in Hilltown, and is the home of the author and winner of the Nobel and Pulitzer prizes. Tours available May through September. For information, call 215-249-0100.

Bikers can obtain maps of routes in the surrounding communities from the Philadelphia Convention and Visitors Bureau, 3 Penn Center Plaza, Philadelphia, PA, 215-636-3300.

GETTYSBURG NATIONAL MILITARY PARK

Gettysburg Park is located in Gettysburg.

Airports

Gettysburg-Doersom, Washington Sectional
Latitude: 39–50
Longitude: 77–16
FSS: 717-774-3626 or 800-692-7471
Gettysburg Cab and Limousine Co: 717-334-1177

York, Washington Sectional
Latitude: 39–55
Longitude: 76–52
FSS: 800-932-0402
Limousine

Climate

Expect hot, humid summers with temperatures ranging from 60° to 90° F. Winters are cold.

Accommodations

In Gettysburg:
Howard Johnson's Motor Lodge, restaurant: 717-324-1188
Gettysburg TraveLodge: 717-324-6235
Best Western-Stonehenge Lodge, restaurant: 717-234-6715
Bed and Breakfast: Hickory Bridge Farm: 717-642-5261

Near the park's tour center:
Gettysburg Holiday Inn, restaurant: 717-334-6211
Heritage Motor Lodge: 717-334-9281
Three Crowns Motor Lodge: 717-334-3168

Camping: Artillery Bridge Campground, Gettysburg KOA, Granite Hill Campground, and Giant

Waterslide. There are also approximately eight campgrounds in the nearby area.

Features

Gettysburg marks the site where on the first three days of July 1863, more soldiers died than ever before in an encounter in the Western Hemisphere. Over 172,000 men were engaged in battle here, making it the "high water mark" in the Civil War. Over 15,000 Confederates charged the Union forces here and lost, thus ending the hope of a successful Northern invasion.

Lincoln delivered his Gettysburg Address at the Soldiers' National Monument on November 19, 1863, in which he said in part: "The world will little note nor long remember what we say here, but it can never forget what they did here."

The battlefield has over 1,100 monuments, statues and markers, three observation towers, and 31 miles of marked avenues.

Cemetery Ridge features the battle headquarters of General George Gordon Meade, commander of the Union forces.

Gettysburg National Cemetery contains the graves of 3,722 Civil War dead, with 979 of them still unknown. Today over 4,000 veterans and their dependents have been buried here and in the nearby annex.

Activities

Gettysburg Tour Center is located at 778 Baltimore: 717-334-6296

Gettysburg Bus Tours takes you for a 23-mile, 2-hour ride around the area, as Raymond Massey and a large cast of Hollywood actors recreate the battle.

Visit Soldier's National Museum, which depicts Charley Weaver and his friends in day-to-day life tableaus of the soldiers.

Gettysburg Battle Theater performs a multimedia reenactment of the battle.

The Jennie Wade House and Old Town have been restored to dramatize the story of Jennie, who was a Gettysburg heroine: 717-334-4100.

Lincoln Train Museum has a Civil War Military Railroad with 1,000 trains, and is open March through November.

Lincoln Room Museum is where Lincoln penned the words of the immortal Gettysburg Address. The room still contains the original furnishings, and the address is presented stereophonically. An admission fee is charged.

Battlefield Tower, 307 feet high, is located across from the visitors center and gives you a panoramic view and an audiovisual program of the battlefield from both enclosed as well as open-air observation decks: 717-334-6754.

Attend a 40-minute presentation on Lincoln in A. Lincoln's Place Theater, adjacent to the Soldier's National Museum: 717-334-6049.

See "The Conflict", the story of the Civil War presented on three screens: 717-334-8003.

Cyclorama offers a 30-minute sound and light program recreating the scene of the fighting.

Explore High Water Mark via a nearby self-guiding trail, or follow the "Bivouac of the Dead Trail." Pick up a Gettysburg Heritage Trail Guide at the visitors center.

See the electric map to get an overall picture of the battlefield.

Take either the 4- or 7-mile special marked bicycle tour.

Special events include the Bluegrass and Apple Blossom Festival, first weekend in May; Civil War Heritage Days, the last week in June and first week in July; Antique shows, the third Saturday in May, and fourth Saturday in September; and the Anniversary of Lincoln's Gettysburg Address, November 19.

Nearby Attraction

Tour the Eisenhower National Historic Site, a century-old farmhouse surrounded by 189 acres of land. Eisenhower lived here until 1969, and Mamie until 1979. Take the shuttle bus from the Tour Information Center.

Information

Superintendent
Gettysburg National Military Park
Gettysburg, PA 17325
717-334-1124

VALLEY FORGE
NATIONAL HISTORICAL PARK

The park is east of Valley Forge.

Airports

Philadelphia-Wings, New York Sectional
Latitude: 40–08
Longitude: 75–16
FSS: 215-673-8020 or 800-822-3750
Rental cars: Budget: 800-527-0700

Pottstown-Limerick, New York Sectional
Latitude: 40–14
Longitude: 75–39
FSS: 215-489-7400

Pottstown Municipal, New York Sectional
Latitude: 40–16
Longitude: 75–40
FSS: 215-489-4080
Car rentals

West Chester-Brandywine, Washington Sectional
Latitude: 39–59
Longitude: 75–34
FSS: 215-692-6710

Car rentals in King of Prussia:
    Avis: 215-265-5755
    Hertz: 215-265-9010
    Budget: 215-492-3900

Climate

The area has cold winters, but has mild temperatures otherwise.

Accommodations

In King of Prussia:
    Holiday Inn-Valley Forge: 215-265-7500
    Budget Lodge at Valley Forge: 215-265-7200
    George Washington Lodge: 215-265-6100
    Howard Johnson's: 215-265-4500

Features

Valley Forge was the camp of General Washington's army during the winter of 1777–78. Despite 2,000 men becoming ill and dying here, by spring, the army was ready to fight the British to a draw at Monmouth Court House in New Jersey.

Activities

Watch a 20-minute orientation film at the visitors center.

Take a self-guided auto tour of the reconstructed huts of Muhlenberg's Brigade, Washington's headquarters, and the log huts occupied by the soldiers. You can also visit reconstructed forts, original entrenchments, and the parade ground. (Fig. 31)

Fig. 31. Arch Monument dedicated to all who served here, Valley Forge.

Narrated 45-minute Valley Forge Park tours leave daily from the visitors center from the end of March until late November.

Washington's Memorial Chapel has relics depicting the history of the country. Next to the chapel is a museum with Revolutionary War momentos. A bell tower with 56 bells is connected to the museum and chapel. The tower presents a concert on Sunday afternoons.

Rent bikes near the visitors center in the park for a 5-mile rolling hills ride through the historic site.

Nearby Attraction

Across the Schuylkill River is Mill Grove, estate of John James Audubon. Tour the museum to see some of his original prints.

Information

Superintendent
Valley Forge National Historical Park
Valley Forge, PA 19481
215-783-7700

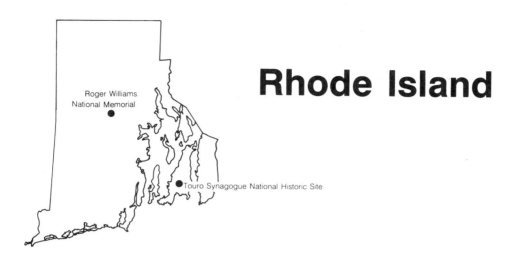

Rhode Island

ROGER WILLIAMS NATIONAL MEMORIAL

The memorial is in Providence at Prospect Terrace on Congdon Street.

Airport

Providence-Theodore Francis Green State
New York Sectional
Latitude: 41–43
Longitude: 71–25
FSS: 800-322-3260
WS: 401-737-3171
Car rentals

Accommodations

Providence Marriott: 800-228-9290
Sheraton Airport Inn, airport transportation, restaurant: 401-738-4000
Howard Johnson's Motor Lodge, airport transportation, restaurant: 401-467-9800

Climate

The summers can be hot and humid.

Features

The monument was established in honor of Roger Williams, founder of the Island Colony and of the town of Providence. His grave is located at the base of the monument.

Williams first came to Rhode Island in 1636 to escape oppression in the Massachusetts Bay Company. He wanted to establish a site where he and his followers could have freedom for religious worship. He named it Providence in "commemoration of God's providence."

Activities

Tour the garden and visitors center.

Visit other historical buildings in Providence, including the old State House built in 1762 and the new State Capitol built in 1900, noted for its large Georgia white marble dome.

The first Baptist Meeting House is located near the Memorial, and was first used in 1683. Many of the other houses have been restored to commemorate life during the 1800s.

See the Slater Mill Historic Site, where a 16,000-pound water wheel built in 1826 is currently operating. Also see early textile machinery and hand-spinning and weaving demonstrations.

Stroll through the Roger Williams Park designed in 1878. Enjoy the rose, Japanese, and Hillside outdoor gardens, and tour the Casino where Providence residents once held many galas. Appointment for tours: 401-785-9450, ext. 59. Tours offered on Monday from noon to 2:00 P.M.

Information

Superintendent
Roger Williams National Memorial
P.O. Box 367, Annex Station
Providence, RI 02901
401-528-4881

TOURO SYNAGOGUE NATIONAL HISTORIC SITE

The site is in Newport at 72 Touro Street and 1½ block east of Colony House on Washington Square.

Airport

Newport State, New York Sectional
Latitude: 41–32
Longitude: 71–16
FSS: 800-242-2377
Car rental

Accommodations

Howard Johnson's Motor Lodge, restaurant: 401-849-2000
Easton's Inn on the Beach, restaurant: 401-846-0310
Newport Harbor Treadway Inn, restaurant: 401-847-9000
Bed and Breakfast of Rhode Island: 401-246-0142
Newport Reservation Service: 401-847-8878

Season

Late June to Labor Day, open 10:00 A.M. to 5:00 P.M. Monday through Friday, and 10:00 A.M. to 6:00 P.M. on Sunday; tours given. The rest of the year, it's open Sunday 2:00 to 4:00 P.M., but you need to make appointment to tour other days.

Features

The synagogue is the oldest one in America and is regarded as one of the most beautiful of America's colonial houses of worship.

The synagogue lost its congregation during the American Revolution, and was used for town meetings and meetings of the General Assembly and the Supreme Court.

Activities

After touring the synagogue, walk up Touro Street to the old burial ground where the Jews important in the history of the synagogue are buried.

Information

Superintendent
85 Touro St.
Newport, RI 02840

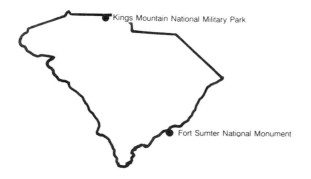

Kings Mountain National Military Park

Fort Sumter National Monument

South Carolina

FORT SUMTER NATIONAL MONUMENT

Fort Sumter is in Charleston Harbor.

Airport

Charleston Executive, Charlotte Sectional
Latitude: 32–42
Longitude: 80–00
FSS: 803-747-5293
INWATS: 800-922-4503
Car rentals

Accommodations

In Charleston:
   Ramada Inn, restaurant: 803-744-8281
   Sheraton Charleston, restaurant: 803-723-3000
   Town and Country Inn, restaurant:
   803-571-1000

In Mt. Pleasant:
   Days Inn, restaurant: 803-881-1800

   Camping: Folly Beach, Ladson, and Johns Island.

Climate

Summers can be hot and humid, while winters are cool and occasionally very cold.

Features

There are two historic sites here: Fort Sumter (Fig. 32) and Ft. Moultrie, a military site.

In March 1861, almost all the forts and navy yards in the seceding states had been seized by the Confederates. However, Ft. Sumter, in Charleston Harbor, remained in Federal possession. The soldiers managed to hold onto the fort 3 months under heavy shelling before surrendering to the Confederates. This led to the eruption of the Civil War.

Ft. Moultrie, located on West Middle Street on Sullivan's Island, was originally constructed for seacoast defense, and was the site of a patriot victory in 1776, when the British were defeated during the Revolutionary War.

Activities

Take a 2½-hour boat tour of Ft. Sumter from the city boat marina on Lockwood Drive. For information and schedules, which vary throughout the year, call 803-772-1691.

Fig. 32. Fort Sumter National Monument. (Photo by R. A. Reilly of Charleston)

Tour the visitors center at Fort Moultrie. A tour of the fort itself will give you a glimpse of how the fort's defense system has changed over its 171-year existence.

While in the area, tour the U.S.S. *Yorktown* in Fort Johnson.

Information

Superintendent
Fort Sumter National Monument
1214 Middle St.
Sullivan's Island, SC 29482
803-883-3123

KINGS MOUNTAIN NATIONAL MILITARY PARK

The park is south of Kings Mountain.

Airports

Charlotte-Douglas International, Charlotte Sectional
Latitude: 35–13
Longitude: 80–56
FSS: 800-222-5743
Car rental

Spartanburg Downtown Memorial, Atlanta Sectional
Latitude: 34–55
Longitude: 81–57
FSS: 800-922-1816
Car rentals

Accommodations

In Charlotte:
   Airport Motel: 803-392-5311
   Holiday Inn: 803-394-4301

In Spartanburg:
   Holiday Inn Spartanburg West, restaurant: 803-576-5220
   Quality Inn, restaurant nearby: 803-585-4311
   TraveLodge: 803-585-6451

Camping: Kings Mountain State Park; none on Tuesdays and Wednesdays.

Fig. 33. Kings Mountain National Military Park. (National Park Service Photo by Richard Frear)

Features

The battle fought here on October 7, 1780, is believed to be the turning point for the American Revolution. The British were defeated by the Tories and brought an increase in American resistance to the British, which ultimately led to the British surrender at Yorktown in 1781 (Fig. 33).

Activities

Visit the ''Living Farm'' in the state park and see a replica of the 1840 frontier farm. It's the site of Frontier Days, a 2-day celebration held in September. Watch competitive shooting and hear authentic folk music.

Swim at a guarded beach in Lake Crawford from Memorial Day to Labor Day.

Hike along a 16-mile trail in the nearby state park.

Cowpens National Battlefield is 18 miles northeast of Spartanburg. Here another battle in the Revolution occurred between Gen. Charles Cornwallis and the Patriots under Nathanael Greene and Daniel Morgan's leadership. Despite the Patriots being outnumbered, they won the battle, sending the British into retreat. The visitor center has a map showing the troops' movements.

Information

Superintendent
Kings Mountain National Military Park
P.O. Box 31
Kings Mountain, NC 28086
803-936-7921

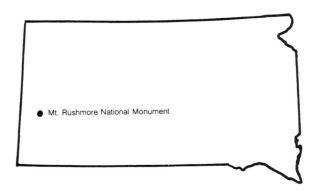

Mt. Rushmore National Monument

South Dakota

MT. RUSHMORE NATIONAL MONUMENT

The monument is 23 miles southwest of Rapid City and 3 miles from Keystone.

Airport

Rapid City Regional, Cheyenne Sectional
Latitude: 44–02
Longitude: 103–03
FSS: 605-342-2280
Car rentals:
   Budget: 605-343-4448 or 800-527-0700
   Hertz: 605-393-0160
   Avis: 605-348-0780
   A-1 Rentals: 605-341-1101
   Thrifty: 605-342-6945

Climate

Summer temperatures average 70 to 90 degrees, cooling off in the evening. Winters average 40°F to −20° F.

Accommodations

In Rapid City:
   Holiday Inn, restaurant: 605-348-1230
   Lake Park Motel: 605-343-1234
   Best Western Town 'N Country Motel, restaurant: 605-343-5583
   Gold Nugget Motel: 605-348-2082

In Keystone:
   Rushmore View Motor Lodge: 605-666-4466
   Powder House Lodge: 605-666-4646
   Four Presidents Motel: 605-666-4472
   Echo Valley Guest Ranch: 605-666-4651 or
      605-666-4836

In Mt. Rushmore:
   Town N Country: 605-343-5383
   Sands Motel: 605-348-1453
   Ramada: 605-342-1300

In Custer:
   Sunset Motel: 605-673-2821
   Rock Crest Lodge: 605-673-4323

In Custer State Park:
   Blue Belle Lodge and Resort: 605-255-4531
   The State Game Lodge: 605-255-4541
   American Presidents Cabins and Camp:
      605-673-3373
   Legion Lake Resort: 605-255-4521

Camping: KOA Campground in Custer, Mt. Rushmore KOA, and Village Campground in Mt. Rushmore: 605-666-8601

Features

In 1927, sculptor Gutzon Borglum was commissioned by the U.S. government to chisel the Shrine to Democracy: the likenesses of the four faces of presidents Washington, Jefferson, Theodore Roosevelt, and Lincoln (Fig. 34).

Washington was selected as father of our nation, and Jefferson as the prime author of the Declaration of Independence and leader in continued growth to the west. Roosevelt was the "trust buster," conservationist, and expansionist, and Lincoln was the emancipator who preserved the union.

The heads of the presidents are between 60 and 70 feet high, with each nose measuring 20 feet, each mouth 18 feet, and the eyes 11 feet across. The figures were scaled to men who would stand 465 feet tall. Borglum and locally trained sculptors chipped away almost ½ million tons of rock from the sunny side of the 6,000-foot peak.

Because the faces have been carved in granite, they will weather away by only ½ inch every 10,000 years.

Activities

The visitors center is open year-round. Food is also available here.

The sculptures are best seen under morning light. Each evening at 9:00 from June 1 to Labor Day

Fig. 34. Faces of four American presidents—Washington, Jefferson, Theodore Roosevelt, and Lincoln—are carved into the 6,000-foot Mt. Rushmore at the Mt. Rushmore National Memorial. (National Park Service Photo by Kenneth Smith)

the sculptures are lit, and an evening program is presented in the amphitheater.

You can also take a park tour. Contact Gray Line of the Black Hills: 605-342-4461; Stagecoach West: 605-343-3113; or Trailways Bus: 605-342-6701.

Climbing of Mt. Rushmore is prohibited. However, rock climbers enjoy climbing the outlet rocks below Sylvan Lake.

Nearby Custer State Park has nine nature trails, ranging from ¾-mile to 12-mile hikes through French Creek Gorge. Sunday Gulch Trail is four miles and passes through the Black Hills.

See the Gordon Stockade, a fort which is a replica of a palisade built in 1874. It's manned with "modern" pioneers who demonstrate the art of making soap and candles and performing other early day chores.

Additional Attractions

Just 22 miles from Rushmore, another giant rock sculpture is being completed. Begun in 1948, a 563-foot mounted figure of Crazy Horse, leader of the Black Hills Sioux, is being worked on. When completed it will be one of the largest sculptures in the world. Crazy Horse is considered to be the "Indian's Indian," who defeated General Custer at the Battle of Big Horn.

Overfly Bear Butte near Sturgis. It's a laccolith, core of an ancient volcano that never erupted.

Attend the Black Hills Passion Play in Spearfish, presented during the summer. It's world-reknowned for its portrayal of the last 7 days of Christ's life. It draws over 100,000 people annually. It's presented Sunday, Tuesday and Thursday at 8:15 P.M. June through August. For reservations, call 605-642-2646.

If you're in Spearfish on a day when the Passion Play isn't being presented, attend the melodrama in the 1906 Matthew's Opera House.

Accommodations

In Spearfish:
Sundance Motel: 605-642-4676
Luxury Lodge: 605-642-2728
Siesta Inn: 605-642-4728 or 800-341-8000; in SD: 800-382-8000
B/B: Sincerely Yours: 605-642-4478

Activities

See the Black Hills Petrified Forest, "Timber of Ages," 1 mile off I-90 near Piedmont exit. Take a guided tour through the only petrified forest in the upper midwest. It's open mid-April through late October. Camping is available: 605-837-2448.

Listen to a concert presented by the Rapid City Municipal band on Wednesday evenings from 8:00 to 9:00.

Drive or bike a 3 percent grade up Spearfish Canyon to see Bridal Veil Falls and Roughlock Falls. Hike to a natural swimming hole, "The Devil's Bathtub." Continue on to Lead to see the largest gold mine in North America.

The Black Hills have 68 of the 72 calcite crystal caves of the world. Nine caves have been developed for public tours.

Information

Superintendent
Keystone, SD 57751
605-574-2523

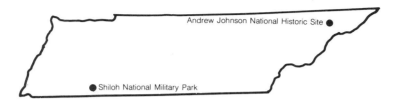

Andrew Johnson National Historic Site ●

● Shiloh National Military Park

Tennessee

ANDREW JOHNSON NATIONAL HISTORIC SITE

The monument is in the northeast part of the Tennessee Valley.

Airports

Greeneville Municipal, Cincinnati Sectional
Latitude: 36–11
Longitude: 82–49
FSS: 800-362-9800
Car rentals
The airport is 3 miles from site.

Tri-City Regional, Cincinnati Sectional
Latitude: 36–28
Longitude: 82–24
FSS: 615-323-6204
Car rentals: Thrifty: 615-323-9181 or 615-926-2277
The airport is 45 miles from site.

Climate

The weather is generally mild with an average annual temperature of 58° F. Annual precipitation is 42 inches.

Accommodations

In Greeneville:
Charroy Inn: 615-638-1331. (You can call collect.)
Holiday Inn: 615-639-4185
King Arthur Motel: 615-638-3151

In Bristol:
Best Western Regency Inn: 615-968-9119
Holiday Inn: 615-968-1101
Comfort Inn: 615-968-2171

Camping is available in five city, county, and state parks.

Features

Andrew Johnson rose through the political ranks beginning with his election as alderman of Greeneville. During the Civil War, he refused to accept the South's position on slavery, and became an advisor on Southern affairs for President Lincoln. In 1864, he was selected to be Lincoln's running mate, and became president in 1865 following Lincoln's assassination.

During his administration, the United States purchased Alaska and successfully applied the Monroe Doctrine against the French in Mexico. Johnson was almost impeached by the House of Representatives for an unpopular decision, but persevered by one vote.

Activities

Since Johnson's father died when he was four, he went to work as an apprentice tailor. Soon he had his own tailor shop, where men would come to read to him as he worked. You can tour this shop along with his two residences and the cemetery in which he is buried.

Greeneville is the site of one of the world's largest tobacco markets. Attend a daily auction except Fridays from November through mid-January. For information, call 638-4111.

Fig. 35. Meriwether Lewis Monument, Natchez Parkway. (National Park Service Photo by John Mohlhenrich)

Nearby Attractions

Boat and fish on the Nolichuckey River or in six other TVA lakes.

Tour Davy Crockett's Birthplace State Park 15 miles northeast of town to see a replica of the cabin in which he was born.

The Johnson home is only 1 hour's drive from the Great Smoky Mountains National Park.

The Meriwether Lewis Monument (Fig. 35) is at milepost 385.9 on the Natchez Trace Parkway: (Fig. 36).

Information

Superintendent
Andrew Johnson National Historic Site
College and Depot Streets
P.O. Box 1088
Greeneville, TN 37744-1088
615-638-3551

SHILOH NATIONAL MILITARY PARK

The park is 10 miles southwest of Savannah, Tennessee.

Airports

Savannah Hardin County, Memphis Sectional
Latitude: 35–10
Longitude: 88–13
FSS: 800-372-8220
Car rentals

Corinth-Roscoe Turner, Memphis Sectional
Latitude: 34–54
Longitude: 88–36
FSS: 601-286-6249
Car rentals

Accommodations

In Savannah, TN:
    Savannah Motel: 901-925-3392
    Shaws Motel: 901-925-3977

Fig. 36. Buffalo River at Metal Ford, Natchez Trace. (National Park Service Photo by Guy Braden)

In Crump, TN:
    River Heights Motel: 901-632-3376

In Pickwick, TN:
    Four Seasons: 901-689-5251
    Bellis Boatel: 901-925-4787

In Corinth, MS:
    Travel Inn: 601-286-5587
    Holiday Inn: 601-286-6071
    Village Inn: 601-286-6695

Features

The area was a major site of the first western battle fought in the Civil War in 1862 between General Johnston's Confederates and General Grant's Union forces. General Johnston was mortally wounded here.

Following 2 days of bitter fighting, almost 24,000 were left dead, wounded, or missing. This battle thus was the worst since the beginning of the war, and the Union buried their dead in the nearby National Cemetery. The Confederates buried theirs in five marked burial trenches.

At the end of the skirmish, the Union had prevailed, and the Confederates were forced to withdraw to Corinth.

The fields and woods look almost the same as they did in 1862.

Activities

Stop by the Visitors Center and watch the 25-minute movie on the battle. Attend Living History programs offered from May through September.

Take a self-guided auto tour of 10 miles.

Walk through the National Cemetery, which overlooks the Tennessee River. Take guided walks to the various sites including Grant's Lost Line, Bloody Pond, and Sunken Road.

Information

Superintendent
Shiloh National Military Park
Shiloh, TN 38376
901-689-5275

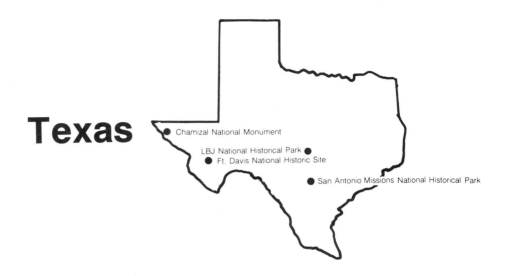

Texas

Chamizal National Monument

LBJ National Historical Park
Ft. Davis National Historic Site

San Antonio Missions National Historical Park

CHAMIZAL NATIONAL MONUMENT

The monument is in the south-central portion of El Paso and is adjacent to the international boundary.

Airport

El Paso International, El Paso Sectional
Latitude: 31–49
Longitude: 106–22
FSS: 915-778-6448
Rental cars:
    Avis: 800-331-1800
    Hertz: 800-654-3131
    Budget: 800-527-0700
Catch a local bus to the park entrance. They run hourly.

Accommodations

La Quinta Motor Inn, restaurant: 915-778-9321
Executive Inn, restaurant: 915-532-8981
Beverly Crest Motor Inn: 915-755-7631

Camping: KOA

Features

The monument commemorates the peaceful settlement of the century-long dispute between the United States and Mexico over the location of the international boundary.

Activities

Tour the visitors center and museum.

Cross the Rio Grande to visit Mexico's park, which offers an outdoor archeological museum, formal gardens, and a museum.

Information

Superintendent
Chamizal National Memorial
P.O. Box 722
El Paso, TX 79444
915-543-7780

LYNDON B. JOHNSON NATIONAL HISTORICAL PARK

The park is 14 miles east of Johnson City and 16 miles from Fredericksburg.

Airport

Fredericksburg-Gillespie County
San Antonio Sectional
Latitude: 30–15
Longitude: 98–54
FSS: 800-292-5493
Car rentals

Accommodations

In Fredericksburg:
    Comfort Inn: 512-997-9811
    Best Western Sunday House Motel, restaurant:
512-997-4333
    My Blue Heaven Motel: 512-997-5545

Camping: Perdernales Falls State Park, Enchanted Rock State Natural Area, Kerrville State Recreation Area, Blanco State Recreation Area, and Lady Bird Johnson Municipal Park, which is adjacent to the Gillespie County Airport.

Features

The park has Texas Longhorn cattle and buffalo near the Sauer-Beckman Homestead. The site features LBJ's boyhood home, with several historic structures and pictures depicting the open range cattle ranching operation of Johnson's grandfather through the more current farming methods.

Activities

From the Boyhood Home located in Johnson City, walk or take a horse-drawn wagon to Johnson Settlement and see the Exhibit Center and Sam Early Johnson Log House. Then drive 14 miles to the LBJ State and National Historical Park at the LBJ Ranch and take a tour bus from the visitors center to see a one-room schoolhouse, birthplace, and family cemetary.

Watch a demonstration of early 1900s farm skills at the Sauer-Beckman Homestead, located 14 miles from the historic park.

In Fredericksburg, visit the Pioneer Museum to see artifacts from the early German immigrants.

Tour Admiral Nimitz Center to see memorabilia from World War II's famous fleet admiral.

Hiking trails available in the Pedernales Falls State Park, Enchanted Rock State Natural Area, and Kerrville State Recreation Area.

Information

Superintendent
Lyndon B. Johnson National Historical Park
P.O. Box 329
Johnson City, TX 78636
512-644-2252

FT. DAVIS NATIONAL HISTORIC SITE

The site is located on the north edge of Ft. Davis, Texas.

Airports

Blue Mountain, El Paso Sectional
Latitude: 30–32
Longitude: 103–59
Note: Private: 915-426-3808

Fort Stockton-Pecos County, San Antonio Sectional
Latitude: 30–55
Longitude: 102–55
FSS: 800-292-5493
Car rentals

Accommodations

In Fort Davis:
    Indian Lodge in the State Park: 416-426-3254
    Limpia Hotel: 416-426-3237
    Stone Village Motel: 416-426-3941

Camping: Davis Mountains State Park.

In Fort Stockton:
    Holiday Inn, restaurant: 916-336-5277
    Silver Saddle Lodge: 916-336-3311
    Rodeway Inn: 916-336-2274

In the Davis Mountains:
    Indian Lodge, restaurant: 915-426-3254

Climate

It's at 4,900 feet and experiences hot summers. Fall is milder. Winters are cool and windy. Spring brings strong winds.

Features

The fort was established in 1854 as a defense post against Indian attacks along the San-Antonio-El Paso Road. The troops stationed here scouted the surrounding territory and escorted mail carriers and travelers passing through Indian territory. It was abandoned in 1891 and had around 70 buildings.

The fort was one of the first in the West to have black soldiers commanded by white officers.

Activities

Tour the visitors center and museum. Half of the original buildings have been restored. Take a self-guided grounds tour.

During the summer, tour the restored officers' quarters. Watch a retreat parade presented every other hour from 10:00 A.M. to 4:00 P.M.

Hike the trails in Davis Mountains State Park. A 4-mile trail connects to Ft. Davis National Historic Site. Hike along additional trails located in the Site.

McDonald Observatory on Mt. Locke offers guided tours. It's located on Skyline Drive. Its 82-inch telescope is the largest in the world available for public viewing. For information, call 916-426-3423.

Drive along 74-mile Scenic Drive, which goes past Davis State Park and McDonald Observatory.

In Ft. Stockton, you can tour historic downtown, including the old fort. Maps are available at the Chamber of Commerce, 222 W. Dickinson. If you drive 20 miles east of town on US 290 and I-10, you'll see a reconstructed stage that was once located along the Overland-Butterfield Stage Route.

Information

Superintendent
Ft. Davis National Historic Site
Ft. Davis, TX 79734
916-426-3225

SAN ANTONIO MISSIONS NATIONAL HISTORICAL PARK

The missions are along the San Antonio River.

Airports

Twin Oaks, San Antonio Sectional
Latitude: 29–34
Longitude: 98–28
FSS: 512-826-9561
Car rentals

Stinson Municipal, San Antonio Sectional
Latitude: 29–20
Longitude: 98–28
FSS: 512-826-8665
Car rentals: Enterprise: 512-224-6363

Accommodations

Hyatt Regency, restaurant: 512-222-1234
TraveLodge on the River, airport transportation, restaurant: 512-226-2271
Holiday Inn-Downtown, restaurant: 225-3211

Features

In the 1700s, a line of Spanish missions was established, stretching from San Juana Bautista in the south to Dolores in east Texas. Each mission then had an Indian village inside, where the inhabitants were given religious and civil training along with instruction in farming, carpentry, and masonry. The missions lost importance as the United States incorporated the western states.

The missions include the San Jose Mission National Historic Site, 6¼ miles south of town; Mission la Purisima Concepcion de Acuna on Mission Rd.; Mission San Francisco de la Espada, 6½ miles south of town; and Mission San Juan Capistrano, 6½ miles south of town.

"The Alamo," the most well-known mission, is a privately run State Historical Site. This mission was begun in 1718, and called the San Antonio de Valero. This is where Col. William Travis, Davy

TAB BOOKS Inc.
Help Us Help You!

So that we can better fill your reading needs, please take a moment to complete and return this card. We appreciate your comments and suggestions.

1. I am interested in books on the following subjects:

☐ automotive
☐ aviation
☐ business
☐ computer, hobby
☐ computer, professional
☐ engineering (specify): _____
☐ other (specify) _____
☐ other (specify) _____

☐ electronics, hobby
☐ electronics, professional
☐ finance
☐ how to, do-it-yourself

2. I own/use a computer:

☐ IBM _____
☐ Apple _____
☐ Commodore _____
☐ Other (specify) _____

☐ Macintosh
☐ ATARI _____
☐ AMIGA _____

3. This card came from TAB book (specify title and/or number):

_____

4. I purchase books:

☐ from general bookstores
☐ from technical bookstores
☐ from college bookstores
☐ other (specify) _____

☐ through the mail
☐ by telephone
☐ by electronic mail

Comments _____

_____

Name _____

Address _____

City _____

State _____ Zip _____

Crockett, and other Texans made their last stand against Mexican General Santa Ana's army of 2,500.

Activities

Get a map of the missions from the park service by writing the superintendent. The missions are still active community centers and churches.

The San Jose Mission is a beautiful Spanish colonial church with a well-known stone carving called Rosa's Window. You can also see the soldiers' barracks and many Indians quarters as they appeared during the time of the Spanish conquistadores. Attend a mariachi mass here.

The Arneson River Theater offers outdoor concerts ranging from jazz and flamenco to opera.

The Spanish Governor's Palace still has furnishings from 200 years ago.

Information

Superintendent
San Antonio Missions National Historical Park
727 E. Durango, Room A612
San Antonio, TX 78206
512-229-6000

Golden Spike
National Historic Site

Utah

GOLDEN SPIKE NATIONAL HISTORIC SITE

The site is 30 miles from Brigham City near the Great Salt Lake.

Airports

Brigham City, Salt Lake Sectional
Latitude: 41–33
Longitude: 112–04
FSS: 800-662-9038

Tremonton Municipal, Salt Lake Sectional
Latitude: 41–43
Longitude: 112–11
FSS: 800-662-9038

Car rentals in town only; none at the airports.

Accommodations

In Brigham City:
    Best Western Motel: 801-723-8584
    Starlite Motel: 801-723-5291
    Red Baron Motel: 801-723-8511

In Trementon:
    Sandman Motel: 801-257-5676
    Marble Motel: 801-257-3524

Features

The railroad was built from the west by Central Pacific and from the east by Northern Pacific. Begun in 1863, the line eventually measured 1,776 miles, and was constructed in less than four years. Central Pacific had the challenge of crossing the Sierra Nevadas, which required cutting 15 tunnels through over 6,000 feet of solid granite. In the great race to lay the most track, resulting in obtaining subsidy bonds, land grants and the Great Basin trade, Central Pacific once laid over 10 miles of track in a day.

Activities

Tour the visitors center and learn about the significance of the nation's first transcontinental railroad. See working replicas of the 1869 locomotives (Fig. 37). Ranger talks are given from Memorial Day through Labor Day.

Take a 9-mile self-guided auto tour of the historic railroad grade, or walk ¾ mile to see the most impressive structural remains.

Information

Superintendent
Golden Spike National Historic Site
P.O. Box Box W
Brigham City, UT 84302
801-471-2209

Fig. 37. Replica locomotives emerge from engine house at Golden Spike National Historic Site. (National Park Service Photo by Marty Lee)

Vermont

Bennington
Battle Monument

BENNINGTON BATTLE MONUMENT

The monument is ½ mile west of Bennington.

Airport

Bennington State, New York Sectional
Latitude: 42–55
Longitude: 73–15
FSS: 800-833-4509
Car rentals

Accommodations

Knotty Pine Motel: 802-442-5487
Harwood Hill Motel, restaurant: 802-442-6278
Paradise Motor Inn, restaurant: 802-442-8351

Features

In 1777, Gen. John Stark and some "Green Mountain Boys" won a decisive victory over the British.

Activities

Climb 412 steps or take the elevator to the top of the monument to see the surrounding countryside.

Visit Old First Church, constructed in 1806, the Jedediah Dewey House, Wallomson Inn, and Isaac Tickenor Mansion, all built in the eighteenth century.

Walk through the Old Burying Ground and Bennington Museum, and hike, swim, and fish in nearby Green Mt. National Forest.

Go through three covered bridges: Silk Road Bridge, Papermill Village Bridge, and Bert Henry Bridge.

Virginia

APPOMATTOX COURT HOUSE NATIONAL HISTORICAL PARK

The court house is in central Virginia, 18 miles east of Lynchburg.

Airport

Lynchburg Municipal-Preston Glenn
Cincinnati Sectional
Latitude: 37–19
Longitude: 79–07
WS: 804-239-5811
FSS: 804-846-6566
Rental cars:
    Rent-A-Car: 804-237-5959
    Rent-A-Wreck: 804-237-7077
    Taxi: 804-352-7007 or 804-352-2421

Accommodations

Traveler's Inn Motel: 804-352-7451
Lee-Grant Motel: 804-352-5234
Holiday Inn: 804-847-4424

Camping: Holliday Lake State Park and Paradise Lake.

Features

The court house is the site where Robert E. Lee, General of the Army of North Virginia, surrendered to Ulysses S. Grant, General-In-Chief of the American forces (Fig. 38).

The original area was called Clover Hill, a stopping-off point on the Richmond-Lynchburg State Road.

Activities

Hike a 5-mile trail past the site of Grant's headquarters and a small Confederate cemetery. The park also has the McLean House, circa 1848, and the Clover Hill Tavern and jail.

Holliday Lake offers fishing, canoeing, and hiking.

Information

Superintendent
Appomattox Court House
National Historical Park
P.O. Box 218
Appomattox, VA 24528
804-352-8987

Fig. 38. Appomattox Court House, Appomattox Court House National Historical Park. (National Park Service Photo by Richard Frear)

BOOKER T. WASHINGTON NATIONAL MONUMENT

The monument is 20 miles southeast of Roanoke.

Airport

Roanoke Regional/Woodrum, Cincinnati Sectional
Latitude: 37–19
Longitude: 79–58
FSS: 800-542-5906
Car Rentals

Accommodations

Econo-Travel Motor Hotel at the Airport, restaurant nearby: 703-563-0853
Howard Johnson's Motor Lodge, restaurant: 703-366-7671
Marriott-Roanoke Airport, restaurant: 703-563-9300

Features

The memorial was dedicated to a former slave who became internationally famous as an educator, speaker, and black leader. He was responsible for seeing Tuskegee Institute become a leading educational institution.

Activities

Follow the Plantation Trail and stop by the various sites to hear an audio message.

Information

Superintendent
Booker T. Washington National Monument
Rt. 1, Box 195
Hardy, VA 24101

FREDERICKSBURG AND SPOTSYLVANIA NATIONAL MILITARY PARK

The park is near Fredericksburg, Virginia.

Airport

Shannon, Washington Sectional
Latitude: 38–16
Longitude: 77–27
FSS: 800-572-6000
Car rentals

Accommodations

In Fredericksburg:
Holiday Inn: 703-371-5550
Fredericksburg Colonial Inn: 703-371-5666
Howard Johnson Motor Lodge: 703-898-1800
or 800-654-2000

Camping is available 23 miles north of town in Prince William Forest, or at the KOA in town.

Features

Spotsylvania was the site of bloody fighting to control the courthouse since the victorious army would then control the shortest route to Richmond. The Union army was commanded by Ulysses S. Grant, and the Confederates by General Robert E. Lee. The hand-to-hand combat was quite intense at Bloody Angle, where for 20 hours the Confederates held the Union forces off and won the skirmish. Approximately 25,000 men fell at the courthouse.

During the eighteenth century, Chatham was home for William Fitzhugh, one of the wealthiest landowners in Virginia. In 1862, it was used as the front-line headquarters for the Union.

The Rising Sun Tavern was built around 1760 by Washington's brother, and was a favorite meeting place for the early patriots.

Activities

Drive along the auto tours of the four battlefields: Fredericksburg, Chancellorsville; Wilderness, and Spotsylvania. Cassette tapes are available.

Take the Fredericksburg Battle Sumkin Road Walking Tour. Hike 4⁷⁄₁₀ miles along Lee Drive. Begin at Howison Hill and go to Prospect Hill.

Hike along the 4-mile Wilderness Battle Trail, or along the Spotsylvania Battlefield History Trail, a 7-mile loop connecting many of the major sites involved in the bitter fighting of May 8 to 21, 1864.

Tour Chatham Manor's historic house and grounds. See a living history program during the summer.

The Fredericksburg National Cemetery contains 15,243 men with 12,700 unknown vets from later wars. It was officially closed in the 1940s.

Visit Kenmore, the colonial home of George Washington's sister, and the Martha Washington house, owned by George's mother. You can also tour the Shannon Air Museum.

See the Stonewall Jackson Shrine in Guinea, VA, a restored plantation office where he died in 1863.

Information

Superintendent
Fredericksburg National Military Park
P.O. Box 679
Fredericksburg, VA 22401

GEORGE WASHINGTON BIRTHPLACE NATIONAL MONUMENT

The monument is 38 miles east of Fredericksburg.

Features

The monument has an historic mansion, colonial farms, burying ground, and hiking trail (Fig. 39).

See Popes Creek Plantation birthplace and the early boyhood home for George Washington. Washington's family were members of the planter aristocracy, which required members to participate in the military and civil affairs of the colonials. The farms were tended by slaves.

The house was built in the 1720s and George lived here 3½ years prior to moving to Little Hunting Creek Plantation, later called Mt. Vernon.

The birthplace home burned Christmas Day, 1776, when Washington was leading the Continental Army in the American Revolution. The plantation was reconstructed and the Memorial House and Kitchen House were built in the 1930s. The original birthplace is still outlined by oyster shells.

Fig. 39. George Washington Birthplace National Monument. (National Park Service Photo by Richard Frear)

Nearby Features

Stratford, Lee's home, adjoins the park on the west. The mansion is one of the grandest colonial homes in America.

Information

Superintendent
George Washington Birthplace National Monument, VA 22575
804-224-0196

MANASSAS NATIONAL BATTLEFIELD PARK

The park is 26 miles southwest of Washington, D.C., near the intersection of I 66 and VA 234.

Airport

Manassas Municipal, Washington Sectional
Latitude: 38–43

Longitude: 77–31
FSS: 800-572-6000
Car rentals:
    Dollar Rent a Car: 703-661-8577
    Ford Rent a Car: 703-491-1131
    Hertz: 703-361-3666

Accommodations

Holiday Inn: 703-361-0131
Econo-Lodge: 703-369-1700
Ramada Inn: 703-361-0221

Camping: Bull Run, Burke Lake, Lake Fairfax, or Silver Lake.

Features

The area is the site of two Civil War battles referred to as First Bull Run and Second Bull Run. The first battle occurred in July 1861, where both sides were seeking to control Manassas, a vital railroad junction, and led to the death of 900 soldiers. It was won by the Confederates.

The second battle occurred in August 1862, and after 3 days of bitter fighting and the death of 3,300, resulted once again in victory by the Confederacy. This second campaign, led by General Robert E. Lee, opened the door for the South's first invasion of the North.

Activities

Walk 1⅖ miles at Stone Bridge and ⅗ miles at Sudley to visit sites on the First Manassas Battlefield. Hike a 1-mile walking tour complete with taped messages and interpretive signs.

The second battlefield covers four times the area, and a 12-mile driving tour takes you past 12 key sites.

Information

Superintendent
Manassas National Battlefield Park
P.O. Box 1830
Manassas, VA 22110
703-754-7107

PETERSBURG NATIONAL BATTLEFIELD

The battlefield is near Petersburg, Virginia.

Airport

Petersburg Municipal, Cincinnati Sectional
Latitude: 37–11
Longitude: 77–31
FSS: 800-582-1013
Car rentals

Accommodations

Ramada Inn: 804-733-0000
Howard Johnsons: 804-732-5950
Holiday Inn North: 804-733-0730

Camping: Lake Chesdin.

Features

The Civil War was 3 years old when the battle occurred at Petersburg. General Lee had set up his headquarters here, and Grant's orders were to destroy this Army of Northern Virginia. A siege of 10 months ensued, the longest in American warfare, and resulted in the loss of 70,000 American lives. Grant cut the railroad supply lines into the city and circled it, forcing Lee to evacuate on April 2, 1865. Lee surrendered a week later at Appomattox Courthouse.

While the siege persisted, Grant replaced his temporary tents with cabins, and eventually 280 structures were constructed along with eight wharves. For a short time, City Point was one of the world's busiest seaports.

Activities

Visit the City Point unit section of the battlefield. Hike along the various trails.

The Petersburg Battlefield Trail is part of the National Recreational Trail System, and offers good hiking.

Drive the 16-mile battlefield tour, which follows most of the Union and Confederate lines built around Petersburg during 1864–65 siege. Stop to take short walks along interpretative trails.

Two hikes include the primary trail tour, a circle hike of 7½ miles, with an optional cutoff shortening it to 4⁷⁄₁₀ miles.

Hike around ¾-mile Meade Station Trail, passing through one of the Union encampments and going to a depot on the military railroad.

The Ft. Stedman Colquitt's Salient Trail is a 1-mile loop, crossing one of the bloodiest spots on the Petersburg Siege line.

Tour the visitors center east of town. A 17-minute map presentation is given hourly. From mid-June through Labor Day, watch the living history program.

The Poplar Grove National Cemetery, 3 miles south of town, has the graves of over 6,000 soldiers.

Tour the old section of the town of St. Petersburg.

Information

Superintendent
Petersburg National Battlefield
P.O. Box 549
Petersburg, VA 23803
804-732-3531

JAMESTOWN NATIONAL HISTORIC SITE

Airports

Williamsburg-Jamestown Airport
Washington Sectional
Latitude: 37–14
Longitude: 76–42
FSS: 800-582-1013
Car rentals

Newport News-Patrick Henry International,
Washington Sectional
Latitude: 37–07
Longitude: 76–29
FSS: 800-582-1013
Car rentals

Bus transportation throughout the restored area is provided by the Colonial Williamsburg Foundation.

Accommodations

Best Western Williamsburg Westpark Hotel, restaurant: 804-229-1134
Holiday Inn 1776, restaurant: 804-220-1776
King William Inn, restaurant: 804-229-4933

Reservations: Williamsburg Hotel/Motel Association's Reservation Service Center; for rooms in a Colonial Home: 800-582-8977 or 804-220-3300.

Camping: There are three campsites near Jamestown, 10 in the Williamsburg area, and four in the Yorktown area.

Features

Jamestown, established in 1609, was the first permanent English settlement in America and was once the capital of the early Virginia Colony. It thrived for almost 100 years despite three fires that destroyed it. After the capitol was moved to Williamsburg, it lost much of its early importance, and not much remains today.

The old Church Tower is the only seventeenth-century structure still standing. However, when you visit the area, you can see old-type brick walls that outline much of the original settlement. Next to many of these walls are paintings that have been erected to show what the area looked like.

Activities

Visitors planning to see both Yorktown and Jamestown may purchase a combination ticket for both in order to save money. Tickets are available at either location.

If you enjoy bicycling, ride to Jamestown from the airport via a quiet secluded and tree-lined road. Go out the airport road to Treasure Island Road and turn left. Follow Treasure Island to Lake Powell Road and turn right. Stay on Lake Powell until it dead-ends at a circular turnaround. Walk your bike across the grassy field to the Colonial Parkway, which is clearly visible ahead of you. Ride approximately one more mile along the Parkway Road into Jamestown.

For a delightful addition to your bike ride, tour the 5-mile circle drive that begins by the visitors center and takes you past a wilderness that is much like it was when the colonists first arrived in 1607. Trails along the road go to Travis Graveyard and to Black Point.

In Jamestown Festival Park, you can visit a reconstructed Indian Lodge to see how the native Americans lived. James Fort has been reconstructed, and you can observe the crafts and trades of the times. A cafeteria is available here. The grounds next to the visitors center contain the ruins of some of the many buildings that once occupied the site.

The Jamestown Museum has one of the most extensive collections of seventeenth-century artifacts in the United States. The Mariner's Museum has the miniature ships of 16 vessels including the *Mora*, sailed by William the Conquerer, and the *Pinta* and *Santa Maria*.

To see a full-scale reproduction of one of the three ships that carried the colonists to Virginia, tour one of them in the harbor at Festival Park. Allow at least one hour.

YORKTOWN BATTLEFIELD AND COLONIAL NATIONAL HISTORICAL PARK

The battlefield is 13 miles from Williamsburg via the Colonial Parkway.

Features

Yorktown was founded in 1691, and was originally a busy seaport. The 1781 Battle of Yorktown was the last major battle fought in the American Revolution. Here, George Washington's army, with the support of French allies, defeated Lord Cornwallis and 7,500 British soldiers.

Today it's most famous for the homes and shops that have been maintained to give the visitor a flavor of life in the 1780s. You can see nine buildings that date back to 1781.

Three blocks from the Victory Center, under the York River, lies one of General Cornwallis' largest warships, the H.M.S. *Charon*, sunk during the Battle of Yorktown. Its hull and contents have been recovered by the Virginia Research Center for Archeology.

A Yorktown shipwreck archeological team is excavating a British supply ship, designated YO88, which was sunk in September 1781 as part of a defensive barrier against a French amphibious landing. A specially constructed pier, located at the foot of Comte de Grass Street, has been constructed to allow visitors to view the excavation.

Activities

Visit Yorktown Village and the Victory Visitor Center to see artifacts collected from the war.

Drive along either the 7- or 9-mile auto tour. Pick up a self-guided leaflet at the visitors center.

The road leads past Washington's headquarters, and his sites of encampments and fortifications. The tour route also includes the Moore House where the British, Americans, and French drafted the terms of the British surrender.

Information

Superintendent
Colonial National Historical Park
P.O. Box 210
Yorktown, VA 23690
804-898-3400

Nearby Attractions

Visit Busch Gardens Old Country Theme Park and the James River Plantations.

WILLIAMSBURG

Williamsburg was carefully planned as the model colonial city, and for 81 years served as the government seat. Then, in 1780, Governor Thomas Jefferson moved the capitol to Richmond.

Activities

Your first stop should be at the Information Center, since tickets must be purchased in advance to visit many of the historic sites in town, including various exhibition buildings and craft shops, Governor's Palace, Carter's Grove Plantation, and Bassett Hall.

In order to see the Governor's Palace, constructed between 1708 and 1720, you should purchase a separate pass, which will have a specific time stamped for your tour.

Restorations in Williamsburg include 88 of the original eighteenth- or nineteenth-century houses, shops, and public buildings. An additional 50 major buildings and many smaller buildings have also been rebuilt on their original sites following extensive archeological, architectural, and documentary research.

Carter's Grove Plantation is located 7 miles east of Williamsburg via the Country Road. The mansion was built in the 1750s and has often been called the most beautiful house in America. It's open from March through November and through the Christmas season.

Although not a part of the historic area, the President's House at the College of William and Mary is another building to visit. The college was chartered in 1693, and is the oldest house of the chief executive of a college in the United States.

You can eat in eighteenth-century tradition by visiting one of the town's taverns, such as Josiah Chowning's Tavern to enjoy Brunswick stew, or eat at King's Arms Tavern to enjoy filet mignon stuffed with Chesapeake Bay oysters.

Because of the closeness of the airport to town, bicycling is an ideal way to see the historic city. There are a couple of downhills from the airport into town, but otherwise the cycling is fairly level. Bikes may be rented in town at Bikes Unlimited, 759 Scotland Street: 804-229-4620, or at Bikesmith, 101-A Penneman Rd.: 804-229-9858.

A 20-mile bike route goes past Colonial Williamsburg and continues to historic Yorktown and Jamestown via the Colonial Parkway. Obtain a map from the VA Dept. of Highways and Transportation, 1401 E. Broad St., Richmond, VA 23219, 804-786-2964.

Klondike Gold Rush National Historical Park

Washington

KLONDIKE GOLD RUSH NATIONAL HISTORICAL PARK

The park is located in the heart of Seattle, 2 blocks north of the Kingdome and 1½ blocks east of the waterfront.

Airports

Boeing Field/King Co. International
Seattle Sectional
Latitude: 47–31
Longitude: 122–18
FSS: 206-767-2726
Car rentals

Seattle-Tacoma International, Seattle Sectional
Latitude: 47–26
Longitude: 122–18
FSS: 206-767-2726
Car rentals: Hertz: 800-654-3131
Most hotels provide transportation from the airport.

Climate

Mild maritime climate. Summer days in the 70s and winter days rarely dropping below the 40s.

Accommodations

Holiday Inn of Sea-Tac: 206-248-1000
Best Western Airport Executel: 206-878-1814
Hyatt Seattle, adjacent to Sea Tac: 206-244-6000
Holiday Inn Seattle-Boeing Field: 206-752-0300

Features

In 1897, one of the last gold rushes in the history of North America left Seattle for the Klondike following word that the Steamship *Portland* had arrived from Alaska carrying over a ton of solid gold.

The big strike in the Klondike had come August 14, 1896, when three men found gold in Rabbit Creek, which empties into the Klondike River. The strike occurred while the country was in the depths of the depression, and Seattle's business doubled and then tripled as thousands of gold-seekers poured into the city.

Prospectors leaving Seattle were advised to take no less than a year's worth of supplies, which cost $300 to $2,000, depending on how much they could afford. Shopowners stocked so many supplies that some stacked their goods 10 feet high along the boardwalks. By the spring of 1898, the merchants had sold over $25 million in goods, with prospectors still arriving.

Pioneer Square has been restored to how it appeared when Seattle was used as the staging area for the gold rush.

Activities

Visit the visitors center to watch films and slides of the gold rush.

Stroll through Waterfront Park, located between Piers 57 and 60.

Tour Pioneer Square. Maps are available at the visitors center.

Nearby Attractions

Tour the Space Needle. It has a variety of restaurants and observation levels. It's open seven days a week. For information, call 206-447-3100.

Tour the Museum of Flight in the restored Red Barn, formerly Boeing's first manufacturing plant, and now a museum on the history of aviation; 9494 E. Marginal Way S.: 206-767-7373.

Visit the Woodland Park Zoological Gardens near Green Lake, open 8:30 A.M. to 6:00 P.M. Information: 206-782-1265.

Information

Superintendent
Klondike Gold Rush National Historical Park
117 So. Main St.
Seattle, WA 98104
206-442-7220

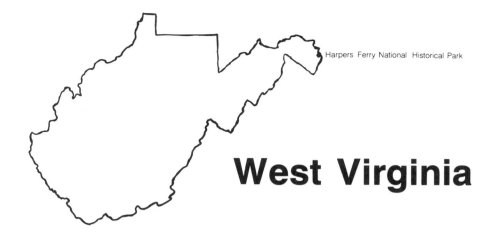
Harpers Ferry National Historical Park

West Virginia

HARPERS FERRY
NATIONAL HISTORICAL PARK

The park is located in Harpers Ferry, West Virginia.

Airport

Martinsburg-Eastern West Virginia Regional
(Shepherd), Washington Sectional
Latitude: 39–24
Longitude: 77–59
FSS: 304-263-9353

Accommodations

Wheatland Motel: 304-267-2994
Ron-De Motel: 304-267-2935
Cliffside Inn: 304-535-6302
Countryside: 304-725-2614

Camping: Sleepy Creek State Park; KOA, open
April 1 to December 6.

Features

In 1794, the U.S. Armory was located in
Harpers Ferry as a convenient access to water
power, and because of the town's proximity to the
nation's capitol. By 1801, the Armory was produc-
ing its first weapons. Some of these were used by
Lewis and Clark on their expedition of 1804–06.

The town has been restored to circa 1859.

Activities

Most action occurs during the summer. You can
see how people lived during the nineteenth century
(Fig. 40). During the spring and fall, park activities
occur on weekends, but the visitors center and
several historic buildings remain open all week.

There are hiking trails in the area. You can picnic and camp near the park, but no facilities are available in the park itself. Close to the park you can hike
along a section of the Appalachian Trail or the C&O
Towpath.

Mountain climbers can scale the cliffs on Maryland Heights. You must register at the ranger station first.

Swimming is not advised because of deep holes
and swift undercurrents. For river rafting, canoeing or fishing, contact the River and Trail Outfitters
at: 301-695-5177.

Nearby Attraction

Visit Crystal Grotto Caverns.

Information

Superintendent
Harpers Ferry National Historical Park
P.O. Box 65
Harpers Ferry, WV 25425
304-535-6371, extension 6222

Fig. 40. Harpers Ferry National Historical Park. (National Park Service Photo)

Blue Mounds State Park ●

Wisconsin

BLUE MOUNDS STATE PARK

Blue Mounds are in the Black River Falls.

Airport

Black River Falls, Green Bay Sectional
Latitude: 44–15
Longitude: 90–51
FSS: 608-784-3170

Accommodations

Best Western-Arrowhead Lodge: 715-284-9471

Features

Blue Mounds is the site of a successful lead mine for Ebeneezer Brigham in the early 1800s. He managed to recover over 1 million pounds of lead from his mine.

When the Indians threatened attack during the Blackhawk War, Ft. Blue Mounds was built for defense.

Activities

Tour Blue Mounds State Park, the highest point in southern Wisconsin. Legend holds that Winnebago treasure has been buried in the mound.

Tour the Cave of the Mounds. Guided tours leave every 15 minutes during the summer. Following your cave tour, hike or picnic on the adjoining Brigham Farm grounds. Attend the annual music festival held during the summer. Concerts include Midsummer Festival, Scandinavian Fiddle Festival, Song of Norway Festival, and Southern Wisconsin Bluegrass Festival. For information, call 608-437-3038.

Nearby is a replica of a church built in Norway for the 1893 World's Columbian Exposition.

ICE AGE NATIONAL SCENIC TRAIL

The trail encompass nine units which include Two Creeks Buried Forest, 12 miles north of Two Rivers; Kettle Moraine, 20 miles west of Sheboygan; Campbellsport Drumlins, 3 miles west of Campbellsport; Horicon Marsh, 1 mile north of Horicon; Cross Plains, 3 miles east of Cross Plains; Devil's Lake, 3 miles south of Baraboo; Mill Bluff in Wildcat Mt. State Park; Chippewa Moraine, 6 miles north of Bloomer; and Interstate, adjacent to the city of St. Croix Falls.

Airports

Sheboygan County Municipal, Chicago Sectional
Latitude: 43–46
Longitude: 87–51
FSS: 414-458-9602
Car rentals: National: 800-328-4567
Provides access to Kettle Marsh.

Bloyer, Chicago Sectional
Latitude: 43–59
Longitude: 90–29
FSS: 608-784-3170
Provides access to Mill Bluff.

Waukesha County, Chicago Sectional
Latitude: 43–02
Longitude: 88–14
FSS: 414-481-1060

Fond Du Lac County, Chicago Sectional
Latitude: 43–46
Longitude: 88–30
FSS: 414-923-0190
Car rentals: Avis: 414-922-6000

Accommodations

In Tomah:
    Holiday Inn: 608-372-3211
    Daybreak Motel: 608-372-5946
    Super 8 Motel: 608-372-3901

In Fond Du Lac:
    Traveler's Inn: 414-923-0223
    Executive Motel: 414-923-2020
    Holiday Inn: 414-923-1440

In Waukesha:
    Holiday Inn: 414-786-0480
    Best Western Motor Inn: 414-547-7770
    Red Carpet Country Inn: 414-547-0201

Camping is available at Fond Du Lac, Whitewater, Campbellsport, and Sheboygan.

Features

The Ice Age National Scientific Reserve was established to preserve the glacial landforms and other features so prominent from the ice age. Over 160 miles of trails have been certified by the Park Service, with another 180 miles uncertified but open to the public. The overall trail design includes 1,000 miles of trails to follow the Southern terminal moraine left by the last Wisconsin glacier. The trails are marked with yellow paint blazes and yellow "Ice Age Trail" signs.

Activities

You can drive to more than one unit in a day: Horicon Marsh, Kettle Moraine, and Campbellsport Drumlins, or go to Devil's Lake and Mill Bluff.

Bikers need to obtain a State Trail permit from the Wisconsin Dept. of Natural Resources in order to ride on the Ahnapee, Sugar River, Tuscobia, Military Ridge, or Drumlins Trails.

Trail heads: Annapee Trail has been established along Lake Michigan at Potawatomi. The Sugar River Trail is east of New Glarus Woods. Proposed links will eventually hook up to established trails near Marathon.

Langlade County contains four established segments ranging from 9 to 14½ miles. Marathon County has five segments with trails ranging from 5¾ to 7¾ miles. Camping is permitted in Eau Claire Dells County Park.

In New Glarus, 19-mile Sugar River State Trail is established. Camp at New Glarus Woods State Park.

In Kettle Moraine northern unit, you'll find a 27-mile trail. Camp at trail shelters. Advance registration is required.

The Ahnapee State Trail is 17 miles long. Chequamegon National Forest has over 100 miles of hiking trails and 26 campgrounds. You can swim from 14 beaches.

Nearby Features

St. Croix Natural Scenic Riverway; Experimental Aircraft Association Headquarters and Museum at Oshkosh.

Information

Superintendent
Ice Age National Scenic Trail
National Park Service
1709 Jackson St.
Omaha, NE 68102

Park Service Information:
Wisconsin Dept. of Natural Resources
P.O. Box 7921
Madison, WI 53707

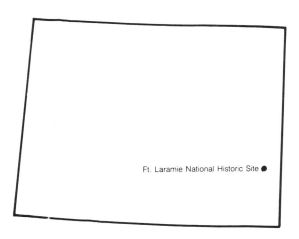

Ft. Laramie National Historic Site ●

Wyoming

FT. LARAMIE NATIONAL HISTORIC SITE

The fort is 3¹⁄₁₀ miles southwest of Ft. Laramie.

Airports

Torrington Municipal, Cheyenne Sectional
Latitude: 42–04
Longitude: 104–09
FSS: 307-635-2615
Car rentals: 307-532-2114
The fort is 23 miles east of town.

Cheyenne, Cheyenne Sectional
Latitude: 41–09
Longitude: 104–49
FSS: 800-442-2965
Car rentals:
    Hertz: 800-654-3131
    Avis: 800-331-1800
    Budget: 800-527-0700

Accommodations

In Torrington:
    Blue Lantern Motel: 307-532-9986
    King's Inn, restaurant: 307-532-4011

Maverick Motel: 307-532-4064
Oregon Trail Lodge: 307-532-2101

In Ft. Laramie:
    Ft. Laramie Motel: 307-837-2360

In Cheyenne:
    Super 8 Motel: 307-635-8741
    Ramada Inn, restaurant, airport transportation:
      307-634-2171
    Holiday Inn, restaurant, airport transportation:
      307-638-4468

Camping in Ft. Laramie at Chuckwagon Drive Inn and Campground, Bennett Court, and K&KL Kampground, 5 miles east of town.

Features

The site has the remains of 21 historic buildings, some dating back to 1849. The fort was operated as a private fur-trading post from 1834 to 1849 and converted to a military post from 1849 to 1890. The fort was located along trails leading to Oregon and California, and was involved in several Indian campaigns.

Activities

Tour the restored buildings, some of which have been refurnished to give a flavor of the historic past. If you tour from June through September, you can witness demonstrations of military and civilian life during the 1870s.

Nearby Features

Near the fort, you'll see an old 1875 Iron Bridge, the only early permanent bridge in the area. You can also see the Grattan Massacre Site, where the 1854 battle occurred between the U.S. Army and the Sioux.

Near Torrington, you can drive past some old ranch houses built in the mid to later 1800s, as well as passing part of the old Oregon and Texas Trails used by the earlier inhabitants who were on their way west.

Information

Ft. Laramie National Historic Site
Ft. Laramie WY 82212-0001
307-837-2221

Trail Guide for Goshen County
Torrington Area Chamber of Commerce
350 W. 21st Ave.
Torrington, WY 82240
307-532-3879

Index

Other Bestsellers From TAB

☐ **ABCs OF SAFE FLYING—2nd Edition—David Frazier**

Attitude, basics, and communication are the ABCs David Frazier talks about in this revised and updated second edition of a book that answers all the obvious questions, and reminds you of others that you might forget to ask. This new edition includes additional advanced flight maneuvers, and a clear explanation of the Federal Airspace System. 192 pp., 69 illus., Hardcover.

Paper $15.95   **Hard $19.95**
Book No. 2430

☐ **ARV FLIER'S HANDBOOK—Joe Christy**

Here's a practical, in-depth look at this increasingly popular new aviation category with a realistic assessment of the ARVs advantages and problems. It includes an overview of the ARV's available today—machines on both sides of the 254 lb./55kt. dividing line. Covered are costs, materials, construction standards, obtaining a license, insurance facts, even cost comparisons with traditional lightplanes. (A "fun" plane that will do 80 mph and costs about $12,000.) 192 pp., 76 illus.

Paper $10.50   **Hard $12.95**
Book No. 2407

☐ **THE ILLUSTRATED HANDBOOK OF AVIATION AND AEROSPACE FACTS—Joe Christy**

A complete look at American aviation—civil and military. All the political, social, economic, and personality factors that have influenced the state of U.S. military airpower, the boom-and-bust cycles in Civil aviation, America's manned and unmanned space flights, and little-known facts on the flights, and little-known facts on the birth of modern rocketry, it's all here in this complete sourcebook! 480 pp., 486 illus.

Paper $24.95   **Hard $29.50**
Book No. 2397

☐ **FLYING VFR IN MARGINAL WEATHER—2nd Edition—Paul Garrison, Revised by Norval Kennedy**

In this revised edition, you'll find technological information on such weather phenomena as wind shear . . . details on today's most advanced lightplane instrumentation including altimeters, airspeed indicators, vertical speed indicators, turn-and-bank indicators, and more . . . tips on the use of wing levelers and autopilots . . . and a practical look at the most advanced new technology in VHF navigation receivers, OBIs, and other navigation equipment including Loran C. 224 pp., 91 illus., Hardcover.

Paper $16.95   **Hard $21.95**
Book No. 2416

☐ **WINGS OF THE WEIRD AND WONDERFUL—Captain Eric Brown**

The Guinness Book of Records lists Captain Eric "Winkle" Brown, the former Chief Naval Test Pilot and Commanding Officer of Great Britain's Aerodynamic Flight at the Royal Aircraft Establishment, as having flown more types of aircraft than any other pilot in the world! Though his test and naval flying writings are already internationally known, he has once more opened his flying logbooks to reveal some of the more unusual types of aircraft. 176 pp., 77 illus.

Paper $15.95   **Hard $19.95**
Book No. 2404

☐ **I LEARNED ABOUT FLYING FROM THAT—Editors of *FLYING*® Magazine**

The editors of *FLYING* Magazine have selected the very best from their publication's most popular regular feature to come up with a series of sometimes humorous, always candid, flying stories. These exciting tales by dozens of high-time pilots—including airman-aerobat Paul Mantz, pilot-author Richard Bach, movie stunt pilots, and many others—all provide valuable flying lessons! 322 pp., 8 illus.

Paper $11.95   **Hard $13.95**
Book No. 2393

Other Bestsellers From TAB